FROM COLONIAL
TO LIBERATION PSYCHOLOGY:
THE PHILIPPINE EXPERIENCE

VIRGILIO G. ENRIQUEZ

DE LA SALLE UNIVERSITY PRESS, INC.
2169 Fidel A. Reyes St., Malate,
Manila, Philippines
2004

Published by
De La Salle University Press
2169 Fidel A. Reyes St., Malate, Manila, Philippines

First Edition 1992
Second Edition 1994 by DLSU Press
    First Printing 1994
    Second Printing 1997
    Third Printing 2004
    Fourth Printing 2006

ISBN # 971-542-002-8

CONTENTS

LIST OF TABLES

LIST OF FIGURES

PREFACE TO THE FIRST EDITION

*F*rom Colonial to Liberation Psychology: The Philippine Experience is an expansion and update of the monograph entitled *Indigenous Psychology and National Consciousness*, which is mainly based on published and unpublished *sikolohiyang Pilipino* materials and documents written in the Filipino language. An English overview of the research literature, historical studies and commentaries in Filipino and English, as well as a description of the philosophy, goals and activities of *sikolohiyang Pilipino* in English, should prove useful to the interested English reader.

In 1987-1988, the Institute for the Study of Languages and Cultures of Asia and Africa, Tokyo University of Foreign Studies, provided generous support to make the writing of a manuscript on the organization of indigenous social psychology concepts of the Philippines possible. The resulting manuscript was the monograph entitled *Indigenous Psychology and National Consciousness*, which tackled both the sociological context of academic indigenous psychology in the Philippines and the substantive organization of indigenous psychology concepts, world-view and values on the basis of an integration of the *sikolohiyang Pilipino* literature and analyses of 1) group interview data using the collective indigenous method, and 2) taxonomic structure of linguistic data using lexical elicitation frames, dictionary entries cross-validated with native speakers of the language, and the subject-index categories of the *Sikolohiyang Pilipino* Resource Collection of the Philippine Psychology Research House.

The support of numerous people and institutions made the research and writing on indigenous psychology possible. The major bases of the present effort included the 1975 articles entitled *Mga Batayan ng Sikolohiyang Pilipino sa Kultura at Kasaysayan* (Bases of Filipino Psychology in Culture and History) and *Sikolohiyang Pilipino: Perspektibo at Direksyon* (Filipino Psychology: Goals and Meaning) delivered at the *Unang Pambansang Kumperensya sa Sikolohiyang Pilipino* (First National Conference on Filipino Psychology) and published as part of the conference proceedings a year later. *Sikolohiyang Pilipino: Perspektibo at Direksyon* was written for the conference which led to the founding of the *Pambansang Samahan sa Sikolohiyang Pilipino*. It was the first formal declaration of the meaning, concepts and goals of *sikolohiyang Pilipino* as an academic discipline of psychology "based on Filipino culture, language and experience." Both articles, written in Filipino, are not yet available in English translation. The earliest article in English, which served as an initial call to indigenization addressed to American-English oriented Filipino social scientists, was entitled "Filipino Psychology in the Third World." It was delivered as a presidential address to the Psychological Association of the Philippines and written while the author was a participant in a program on cross-cultural research for behavioral and social scientists at the East-West Center in Honolulu, Hawaii in 1977. The address also served as a predecessor providing direct basis for the present effort.

The opportunity to write Chapters 1-3 on the colonial background of psychology in the Philippines and the subsequent development of psychological thought in the country was provided by the Southeast Asian Studies Program, Institute of Southeast Asian Studies, through a research and teaching fellowship at the University of Malaya, Kuala Lumpur, in 1983-1984. The historical aspects of Philippine psychology incorporated in said chapters of the book were taken from an article entitled "Decolonizing the Filipino Psyche: Philippine Psychology in the Seventies," published in the *Philippine Social Sciences and Humanities Review* in 1981 and reprinted by the Philippine Psychology Research and Training House in 1982. Said article was revised and expanded with a new subtitle: "Decolonizing the Filipino Psyche: Impetus for the Development of Psychology in the Philippines" under the editorship of Geoffrey H. Blowers and Allison M. Turtle and included in an anthology *Psychology Moving East: The Status of Western Psychology in Asia and Oceania*, published by Westview Press, Inc. in Boulder and London in 1987. The earlier manuscript version of Chapters 1-3 was revised, expanded, updated and subsequently published as Teaching and Research Exchange Fellowships Report No. 3 entitled *From Colonial to Liberation Psychology: The Indigenous Perspective in Philippine Psychology* while the writer was a Visiting Research Professor at the Institute for the Study of Languages and Cultures of Asia and Africa, Tokyo University of Foreign Studies.

In particular, Chapter 2, entitled "The Meeting of East and West" was based primarily on interviews and knowledge acquired in the course of teaching in the Philippines at the University of the Philippines, De La Salle University, Centro Escolar University, Pamantasan ng Lungsod ng Maynila and the University of Santo Tomas. The direct cooperation of numerous people from other institutions, particularly, the Ateneo de Manila, University of San Carlos and the St. Louis University, was also most helpful. They all consented to share their experiences as practitioners, professors and social science researchers. The National Research Council of the Philippines supported visits to the above-mentioned universities and research institutions throughout the Philippines, as well as numerous others including Xavier University in Cagayan de Oro and Aquinas University in Legazpi. The findings from a good number of other colleges and universities were not directly cited in the present manuscript but the cooperation and invaluable assistance of professors, students, librarians and non-academic staff made the completion of this book possible. I have to mention two of my research associates, Elizabeth Pastores, who, in the characteristic fashion of trained historians, patiently and thoroughly organized the materials which formed the core of the library collection of the Philippine Psychology Research House, and Abraham Velasco, who went to research institutions no matter how difficult the travel conditions were, thus taking advantage of his background as a forester, in search of documents and people who can throw light as well as help build a Filipino-oriented psychology.

I gained a closer view of the immediate past of psychology in the Philippines, of events prior to the advent of *sikolohiyang Pilipino* as a movement, through interviews with A. V. Hartendorp in the intimacy of his home in San Juan, Rizal and by listening to Agustin Alonzo, whom we invited to talk on the topic in the graduate seminar class on the History of Psychology which I handled at the University of the Philippines in 1973. I also had the privilege of conducting a taped interview in his office at the Manuel L. Quezon University apart from supervising a research on Agustin Alonzo done by my student, Eleanor Sarra, for her History of Psychology class. Joseph Goertz described his work at the University of San Carlos in Cebu City in a formal interview in 1973 in connection with my research integration project on Philippine Psychology supported by the National Research Council of the Philippines and the Philippine Social Science Council. Both Fr. Goertz and Fr. Fertal provided a wealth of information on early developments in academic psychology at the University of San Carlos by consenting to an interview. The informal exchange and pleasant visits with the young faculty of the department up to the mid-'70s makes one wistful of friendships obstructed only by distance and time. A visit to Evarist Verlinden and the Psychology Laboratory at St. Louis University in Baguio City in 1974 provided the information on developments in psychology in Northern Philippines. Jaime Bulatao also consented to an interview in his office at the Ateneo de Manila Psychology Department in 1984. The Department of Psychology, University of the Philippines was particularly hard to handle because of my direct involvement in the affairs of the department which nurtured many of the names and ideas tackled in this book. The task of writing about psychology at the University of the Philippines was easiest whenever I was out of Philippine soil. Ironically, I learned a lot more about the U.P. Department of Psychology while I was in Honolulu and Hong Kong.

While the concept of a *sikolohiyang malaya at mapagpalaya* is integral to the *sikolohiyang Pilipino* perspective and has been used as early as 1971 and in the *Linggo ng Kasaysayan* (History Week) celebration at the University of the Philippines in 1972, *Liberation Psychology* as an English translation for *Sikolohiyang*

Mapagpalaya was extensively used for the first time in 1984 in my heated discussions with Elizabeth Protacio Marcelino on the English interpretation of my thesis on psychology and language written in Filipino. The task of sharing in English the *sikolohiyang Pilipino* concepts and ideas originally articulated in Filipino was by no means easy. It was made pleasant only through the invaluable help of Elizabeth Protacio Marcelino's husband Alex Marcelino, who was a political prisoner of the Marcos dictatorship in Camp Bicutan at the time.

The term *"liberation psychology"* gained deeper significance in 1986 even in the air-conditioned classrooms of De La Salle University as Marcos loyalists disputed the prevailing sentiment denouncing Marcos' ignominious attempt to rig the snap elections. The De La Salle University campus banner exalting freedom and justice was hurriedly taken down, folded and kept upon the flight of the dictator to the United States of America. The conditions which made the concept of *liberation psychology* meaningful stayed, nevertheless. The struggle goes on.

Sikolohiyang mapagpalaya was further examined as *liberation psychology* in my class on the Theoretical and Historical Foundations of Psychology at De La Salle University. This was mainly because of one American student in class who was willing to listen to lectures in Filipino, so I accommodated him by summarizing my lectures in English and by occasionally lecturing in English as well. My graduate class on the Development of Psychological Thought at the University of the Philippines in 1987 was also the venue for further refining a *liberation psychology* required by the internal contradiction between the masses and the elite in Philippine society. A conflict model was not necessarily endorsed by the recognition of a cultural divide. In fact, the prevailing mood which went with welcoming the "democratic space" afforded by the Aquino regime was anchored on the pressing task of nation building.

In December 1987, a conference organized by Setsuho Ikehata of the Institute for the Study of Languages and Cultures of Asia and Africa, Tokyo University of Foreign Studies provided the opportunity for the presentation of my working paper on the concept of *katarungan* (justice) in the Philippine value system which served as a major basis for Chapter 4. The working paper was based on field studies in Bulacan, Diliman, and Laguna with the support of the Department of Local Governments, Republic of the Philippines, through the De La Salle University and the Philippine Psychology Research and Training House. The new interpretation of the Filipino personality and values in Chapters 4-5 is primarily an expansion and update of the portions of the working paper on *katarungan* relevant to the structure of the Philippine value system using the indigenous language as a resource. Chapter 4 was revised on the basis of questions and comments raised in the 1987 Conference of the Institute for the Study of Languages and Cultures of Asia and Africa. Work on the structure of the indigenous value system started much earlier, in 1984 to be exact, in preparation for my year of writing as Visiting Research Professor at the Tokyo University of Foreign Studies three years later.

At the core of the Philippine value system is the concept of *kapwa*. The paper entitled *"Kapwa*: A Core Concept in Filipino Social Psychology" was written for the 20th Annual Conference of the Japanese Society for Social Psychology on "Key Concepts of Psychology in Asia" held in Mitaka, Tokyo, Japan upon the invitation of Professor Akira Hoshino of the International Christian University. The paper was included in the antedated 1978 issue of the *Philippine Social Science and Humanities Review*. The structure of the Philippine value system beyond the core concept of *kapwa* was further developed for the Symposium on Social Values and Development in the Third World Countries at the University of Hong Kong in 1987. The resulting article was entitled "The Structure of Philippine Social Values: Towards Integrating Indigenous Values and Appropriate Technology." A version of the paper was published in the Philippine magazine for educators, *Tagsibol*, under the title "Filipino Values: Towards a New Interpretation" that same year.

The discussion of *indigenization from within* as found in Chapter 6 was first presented formally at the First Regional Conference on Cross-Cultural Psychology held at the University of HongKong on March 19-23, 1979 and published in the *Philippine Journal of Psychology 12*(1), 9-15. I acknowledge with thanks the comments made by Robert Serpell, Juris Draguns and Victoria Bunye on the earlier version of that paper.

Chapter 7 on liberation psychology and the national culture is a brief description of the events and issues crucial to the development of a consciously indigenous scientific psychology in the Philippines. The discussion of Martial Law and related events was taken from "The Philippines: From Marcos to Aquino," a paper I presented at the International Institute of Communication's 21st Annual Conference in Dublin, Ireland on September 12-15, 1990. I had the special advantage of witnessing many decisive events which forged the direction of the indigenous social science movement in the country, especially in psychology, anthropology and applied linguistics. Working with colleagues at the *Pambansang Samahan sa Sikolohiyang Pilipino,* the National Research Council of the Philippines, the Language Education Council of the Philippines and the Philippine Social Science Council also afforded many opportunities for actively observing the forces that direct the growth of indigenization in Philippine Social Science.

The monograph on *Indigenous Psychology and National Consciousness* was presented for discussion to the Faculty of the Institute for the Study of Languages and Cultures of Asia and Africa on September 14, 1988. Important questions relating to the issue of ethnic heterogeneity of the Philippines were raised, prompting me to decide on a separate section on ethnic diversity in Chapter 3. The discussion on *kapwa* psychology in Chapter 4 had to be extended to cover its meanings throughout the Philippines. What is interesting to note is the observation that *kapwa* as a concept appears to extend even to other countries, including Japan. Still, there is a need to verify whether the value of *kapwa* indeed obtains throughout the Philippines.

I was cut from the mainstream of events and developments in Philippine indigenous social science while teaching and researching at the University of Hong Kong briefly in 1982 and at the University of Malaya at Kuala Lumpur, Malaysia for academic year 1983-1984 and while working on this book at the Tokyo University of Foreign Studies in 1987-1988. Being away from "where the action is" is difficult but I was partly rewarded with the much-needed measure of objectivity afforded by distance. But I must say that I was concerned when told by a well-meaning colleague in Japan that "there is no Philippines." Apparently the comment was to be interpreted from the anthropological point of view which emphasizes the "cultural heterogeneity" of the Philippines and the Filipino sense of nationhood or alleged absence thereof. I am not comfortable with this view even from the very same vantage point of anthropology and social science. In any case, part of the task ahead is demonstrating that indeed "there is a Philippines" not just by way of a social science exercise but also through concrete action on the part of Filipinos, including scholars.

I extend my heartfelt thanks and appreciation to the institutions and individuals who made this book possible:

The Institute for the Study of Languages and Cultures of Asia and Africa, Tokyo University of Foreign Studies, for permission to publish the revised and expanded version of the monograph entitled *Indigenous Psychology and National Consciousness* in book form in the Philippines; the De La Salle University Press for agreeing to publish this work; Jose Ma. Bartolome and Eduardo Muñoz Seca for the photographs used in this book; Ann Barbut and Sylvia Ventura for the valuable comments on the language of the final manuscript; and Oliver S. Trinidad and Teddy V. Angel for their invaluable assistance in preparing the manuscript for publication.

VIRGILIO G. ENRIQUEZ

PREFACE TO THE SECOND EDITION

This edition of *From Colonial to Liberation Psychology: The Philippine Experience* includes a discussion of Filipino Psychology as an international movement and a brief documentation of the more recent efforts towards the decolonization of the psyche of the Filipino. Minor changes were made including the rearrangement of the glossary entries, addition and correction of some reference entries, and the use of uniform size and types for the Tables and Figures. Some pictures were replaced with clearer and even more appropriate ones.

When this book was published last year we did not expect the interest it would generate and that we would run out of copies in a matter of months. That is why the book is reprinted by the De La Salle University (DLSU) Press with the permission of the author and the University of the Philippines Press.

Several reactions and comments were made during the launching of the first edition of the book. Commending the author for being on the forefront in propagating *sikolohiyang Pilipino*, Isagani R. Cruz of the De La Salle University (DLSU) pointed out that this book "documented the dramatically successful movement to decolonize Philippine life thereby liberating psychology from inapplicable Western models." He added that the book also shed fresh insights into concepts like *hiya, pakikisama, utang na loob* and that although psychology can be technically correct only if done in a local language, he said Enriquez did a "good job of approximating in English the insights of our psychologists."

Albert Alejo of the Ateneo de Manila University was not as lavish in his assessment, and raised the issue on why the book, which supposedly espouses and asserts Filipino identity, decolonization and indigenization, was written in English, and not in Filipino. He reported that while his attention was diverted from reading the book when he saw someone reading a sex advice column in one of the tabloids, hardly anyone paid any attention to the book he was reading. The message was clear and unmistakable: the book, written in English, is not easily understood by the masses hence, its reach, accessibility and effectiveness are limited by the language barrier.

Sikolohiyang Pilipino publications are primarily in Tagalog but Alejo's assessment is well taken. Just the same, there is no need to share Sikolohiyang Pilipino in English for it to be understood by English readers. Sikolohiyang Pilipino has taken on an international character and monographs and articles are now available in foreign languages including a Ph.D. dissertation in German.

Political Scientist Jose V. Abueva, for his part, stresses that by offering a refreshingly healthy view of traditional Filipino values, which Westerners branded as negative traits, Enriquez helped ''elevate the Filipino image, boost his self-confidence, and reaffirm his innate strength of character which can be his very instrument for liberation from his colonial psychology.'' By adopting a pro-Filipino stance in this book, Abueva said Enriquez's works challenge other social scientists to conduct studies with the end view freeing the Filipino mind from colonial values and biases.

16 November 1993
Quezon City

INDIGENOUS PSYCHOLOGY
AND NATIONAL CONSCIOUSNESS

Psychology as an academic discipline and profession in Asia is usually viewed as continuous with the development of psychology in the West. As a field of knowledge, psychology has been treated historically by Western psychologists (e.g.,Boring 1929, Watson 1963) and their accounts of psychology as a modern science usually begin with the establishment of the experimental psychology laboratory in 1879 by Wilhelm Wundt in Leipzig, Germany. Western historians trace the development of psychological thought to the Greek philosophers. Aristotle's *De Anima* is often considered a start in tracing the roots of psychology as a human concern. It must be noted, however, that historians of psychology consciously or unconsciously drop the word "Western" when they write about the history of Western psychology. On the other hand, Asian psychology (e.g., Murphy and Murphy, 1972) is always properly designated as such: Asian.

Reference to Asian psychologies is not new at all. Psychologists also talk about Chinese psychology, Indian psychology, and Philippine psychology, for example. What should be made clear, however, is that they usually mean psychology in China, India or the Philippines in the Western tradition and not Chinese psychology, Indian psychology, or Philippine psychology in the Chinese, Indian or Philippine tradition. It is no surprise then that Westerners feel at home writing about the "psychology of, by and for" natives of a Third World country such as the Philippines without being immersed in the native culture or at least having learned the local language.

All these could very well be a product of a well-meaning interest in a former colonial country or a commitment to the development of psychology as a field of

1

knowledge. The fact remains that the history of psychology has to be rewritten indeed so as to reflect the different bodies of knowledge, formal or informal, found in Asia and the different cultures of the world. If this is not done, what one has is at best a history of psychology which ignores the traditional roots of psychological thought in Asia--a history of Western psychology with the word "Western" unsaid or unwritten.

The development of psychological thought has a long history and many filiations in Asia and the rest of the world. The Philippines is no exception. To be sure, one finds psychology in the practice of the *babaylan* and *catalonan* in the Philippines but just the same, most academic departments of psychology in Philippine universities tended to ignore indigenous psychological thought and practice and instead adopted theories, methods and practices from their Western counterparts. It is only lately that more and more Filipino psychologists have come to appreciate the need to recognize the indigenous roots and contemporary social and behavioral manifestations of a "less civilized" psychology hand in hand with the awareness of the Western influence in the development of psychological thought in Asia. The value placed on modernity and development leads some to conclude that whatever is indigenous is uncivilized, making the word "indigenization" dirty. "Contextualization" as a label is thus preferred over "indigenization."

Actually, the word "indigenization" is not as politically charged as it appears in many cases. "Contextualization" sounds neutral but it took the form of decolonization and "indigenization" in Philippine psychology regardless of one's dissatisfaction with the word. The Filipino word *pagsasakatutubo* captures the situation aptly even if *pagsasakatutubo* is a tongue twister for the American-trained Filipino scholar. The ultimate goal of *pagsasakatutubo* is a *sikolohiyang malaya* and *mapagpalaya* (i.e., a *liberation* psychology): *malaya* (literally, "free," "independent," and "liberated") or unshackled by the massive American political, economic and cultural influence in Philippine life, society and psychology, and *mapagpalaya* (literally, "liberating") or responsive to internal Philippine social problems primarily rooted in the inequitable distribution of wealth and the Great Cultural Divide separating the Anglicized Filipinos from the masses.

1

A HISTORICAL BACKGROUND

The Republic of the Philippines comprises 7,107 islands located at the western edge of the Pacific Ocean, east of Vietnam, south of Taiwan and north of Sabah in Malaysia. There are approximately 60 million multi-ethnic and multilingual Filipinos who are primarily Malayo-Polynesian. However, a good number of them look more *Chinito* (or Chinese), *Bumbay* (or Indian), and *Tisoy* (or Spanish), in various degrees.

For the purpose of tourist promotion, the Philippines is billed as the "third largest English-speaking country in the world." In fact, English is understood and spoken by Filipinos who went through American-oriented schools with English as the medium of instruction. However, one has to reckon with the heavy accent in *"Tenkyu beri mats."*

The new Philippine Constitution of 1987 retained the English language as an official language but it is the Filipino language that is used across the archipelago by the man-on-the-street on the other side of the Great Cultural Divide. Legalistic members of the elite refuse to acknowledge the existence of a Philippine national language; writers and language scholars argue over the difference between Pilipino and Filipino; and the University of California-trained Filipino teachers of English argue passionately for the colonial language. But the fact remains that the language of the Philippine masses is the language of the Philippines.

The dominant home-grown religion is the *Iglesia ni Kristo*. The historian Agoncillo (1974) explains:

> Like the Philippine Independent Church, the Iglesia ni
> Kristo is by the masses. The masses who belong to the

3

Catholic Church are superficial Catholics, while those belonging to the Iglesia are devoted followers and loyal adherents
of their Church...The Catholics, it is true, go to church on
Sundays and holidays, but they do so not because they understand and appreciate the mysticism and poetry of the Catholic
rites, but because it is the fashion to be seen in the Church on
such days. And so, while statistics show that Catholics
comprise 83 percent of the total population, actually the
genuine Catholics do not probably comprise 0.5 percent of the
whole population.

The Christianized animists form a majority in the Philippine islands of Luzon and
Visayas but the Catholic church plays a vital role in Philippine economy and polity. To be
sure, the friar lands have been gradually transferred since 1903 from the Catholic Church
to the government and private hands but the religious orders have a long way to go before
they can make good their vow of poverty in the islands. The Spanish Dominican priests are
still embroiled in a struggle with Filipino priests for financial control of the University of
Santo Tomas, the oldest Catholic university in the Philippines. The struggle surfaced anew
just after Filipino consciousness was shaken by the historic assassination of Benigno
Aquino at the Manila International Airport in 1983. Jaime Cardinal Sin, leader of the
Filipino Catholics, appealed for "reconciliation with justice" as the nation recoiled from
the shock of a politically motivated murder which ignited the spark leading to the fall of a
dictator and a change in leadership.

Islam is dominant in Southern Philippines as it is dominant in neighboring Malaysia
and Indonesia. Regardless of what the future has in store for the Moro National Liberation
Front, the Mindanao calendar includes the Hari Raya Puasa on top of the more familiar
Christian holidays in Luzon. Just the same, Filipino religious psychology is best found in
Islamized animism or Christianized Bathalism (from the name *Bathala,* or God) but the
traditional indigenous religion, Anitism (from the word *anito*, or ancestral god), and respect
for nature, are deeply held in various aspects of life.

Early Philippine Psychology

The psychological knowledge of the native Filipino traditionally held by the
babaylan in the Visayas, the *catalonan* in Central Luzon, and the *baglan* in the Northern
Philippines (Bailen 1967, Quiazon 1973), is an important basis of early Filipino
psychology. The *babaylan* was the first Filipino psychologist. As a priestess she was also
the guardian of Filipino sacred knowledge. In the early days she did not refer to herself as
Filipino but nonetheless continued her practice as *babaylan* through the centuries of
identity evolution from *Indio* to Filipino. The *dalangin* (prayer) and *bulong* (whisper) of
the *catalonan* and other healers and priestesses from different ethnic groups in the

Philippines are rich sources of early Filipino psychology. The use of *anting-anting* (amulets) and other psychological practices and beliefs of resistance movements such as the Pulajanes (Constantino 1975) are all rooted in early Filipino psychology.

Part and parcel of early Filipino psychology is the psychology found in early Philippine literature, be it oral or scribbled on bamboo: the *salawikain* (proverb) (Eugenio 1966), the *bugtong* (riddle), the *kuwentong bayan* (folk tales), the *alamat* (myth) and the *epiko* (epic).

The inherited customs of the Filipino serve as one of the fundamental bases of Filipino psychology. Related to this is the rich field of ethnopsychology. Handed from generation to generation are the beliefs and practices on childcare (Abasolo-Domingo 1961, Quisumbing 1964, Aldaba-Lim 1966, Temporal 1968, Almendral 1969, Adea 1974, Lagmay 1974, Alonto 1975) and the intricate knowledge which governs interpersonal relationships (Gutierrez-Gonzales 1968, Almario 1972, Nuevo 1973). The Filipino psychologist cannot gain this knowledge in New York, Paris or Munich. It is best that the psychologist actually live in the barrio where he came from in order to learn and rediscover Filipino psychology.

Filipino psychology is the attachment of importance to the Filipino and his consciousness. The totality of the Filipino--both his material and spiritual aspects-- are given emphasis. This perspective, labelled *sikolohiyang Pilipino*, motivates the social scientist to investigate the traditional beliefs of native Filipinos.

A turn of events encouraged Zeus Salazar (1974), historian and ethnologist, to study the belief in two souls: *diwa* (consciousness) and its counterpart. Salazar identified four lines of history and filiation of Philippine psychology, namely the academic-scientific psychology, the academic-philosophical psychology, ethnic or indigenous psychology, and the psycho-medical psychology with Filipino religion as the cohesive element. Academic-scientific psychology, which has a direct filiation with Wilhelm Wundt, found its way to the Philippines primarily through the University of San Carlos in 1954 and the University of the Philippines in 1920 with the establishment of the American educational system in the Philippines. The Filipino phase of academic-scientific psychology began with the return in 1925 of Filipino pioneers in Western psychology belonging to the pragmatist-behavioral school which had just then begun to distinguish itself from its European origins mainly the German, English and French traditions. The academic-philosophical psychology, for its part, traces its roots to the establishment of a system of higher education at the University of Sto. Tomas in Spanish times in about the middle of the 17th century.

The third, ethnic psychology, otherwise called *katutubong sikolohiya* or indigenous psychology, is a psychological system worked out by Filipinos from indigenous and foreign elements in response to their national and cultural experiences.It includes the study of Filipino psychology in the context of the Filipino people's perceived ethnic traits which may be culled from both native or foreign, mainly Spanish, sources. Filipino psychology attempts to study psychology in the Philippine context and with a Filipino orientation with the end in view of countering foreigners' negative perceptions of Filipinos. It involves the study of Filipino ethnic psychology from the early times up to the present. Finally, the psycho-medical system with religion as the cohesive element and explanation can be considered to be at the core of native Filipino psychology. It is manifested through faith healing connected with the *espiritista* movement and techniques of healing through *herbolaryo* and other indigenous methods. A diagram of the four lines of filiation as drawn by Salazar is shown in Table 1.

A distinct and important line of filiation showing the roots and development of the economic, livelihood, agricultural, business, management and industrial psychology is currently conceptualized around *sikolohiyang pangkabuhayan* ("livelihood" psychology). Great interest in the indigenous arts also motivates work on the traditional and contemporary people's arts, thus leading to intensive research and artistic activities in *sikolohiya ng sining* (psychology of art).

The Indigenous Psychological Tradition

The psychology of the victorious Lapu-Lapu, who epitomized Filipino courage and tradition, is an important topic for a Filipino-oriented psychological research and study. Western-oriented historians tend to give inordinate attention to visitors of this country. The *sikolohiyang Pilipino* historian, however, pays greater attention to history from the indigenous point of view. For instance, he looks at Manila under the rule of Lakan Dula of Tondo, or of Rajah Sulaiman of Maynilad, who earned the reputation of being "the greatest chief of all that country with whom the terms of peace and friendship were to be made" (Quirino 1981).

The social psychology of the indigenous culture, rights and practices was staunchly protected by Diego Silang of Ilocos, and upon his death by his wife Gabriela Silang, whose name is now a rallying cry for the Filipino women. Although Diego Silang was later assassinated and his wife hanged in a public plaza, they without doubt helped keep the flame of indigenous pride and unity burning. The understanding of indigenous Filipino psychology can also deepen by examining the lives, convictions and ideas of Tamblot and Dagohoy of Bohol. Tamblot, a *babaylan* or native psychologist-priest, kept the sacred tradition by establishing a major Visayan leadership in 1621, refusing to pay tribute to any foreign adventurer. The Boholanos, for their part, enjoyed one of the longest periods of local sovereignty in Philippine history, from 1744 until 1828, blessed with the Filipino concept of justice, equality and liberty under the leadership and authority of Francisco Dagohoy and his successors. The great following of Apolinario de la Cruz, more popularly known as Hermano Pule of Lukban, Tayabas, attested to his religious charisma and the local validity of his psychology. The decades prior to the establishment of the first Philippine Republic in Kawit, Cavite on June 12, 1896 were documented with historical accounts rich in psychological content. In fact, this period witnessed the tremendous surge of psychological renewal.

TABLE I

FOUR FILIATIONS OF PHILIPPINE PSYCHOLOGY

	1565	1650	1730	1900	1920	1970
I. ACADEMIC-SCIENTIFIC PSYCHOLOGY: THE WESTERN TRADITION				1876: Birth of Scientific Psychology (German tradition)		Entry of Western Psych. (U.P. and other Universities); mainly American tradition
II. ACADEMIC-PHILOSOPHICAL PSYCHOLOGY: THE WESTERN (MAINLY CLERICAL) TRADITION	U.S.T., and later other schools of higher education. Individual monks and preachers: The **Jesuits**; **Thomistic Philosophy** and **Psychology**. Continuing study of psychology as an aspect of philosophy.					
III. ETHNIC PSYCHOLOGY:	**Sikolohiyang Etniko** as major basis of Sikolohiyang Pilipino for integrating I and II into a national tradition of **Psychology** and **Philosophy** as universal disciplines.					
A. *Indigenous Psychology* (Katutubong Sikolohiya: indigenous psychology in the sense of):						
1. Common to the Filipinos who oftentimes are unaware of it: this frame of psychological reason or theory can be culled principally from language, literature, etc. but only as principles (specifically, this can be called **kinagisnang sikolohiya**).						
2. Psychologies or psychological systems worked out by Filipinos with indigenous elements as basis. Example: **Hermano Pule, Rizal, Isabelo de los Reyes, Kalaw, Mercado, Alejo,** etc. Mainly reactive, resulting from contact with other cultures and from acculturative experience. **Katutubong Sikolohiya** *per se.*						
B. *Psychology of Filipinos* (as observed by foreigners or as felt and expressed by Filipinos):						
1. Based on mainly Western System of thought: Chinese, Spaniards, then other foreigners.		**Colin and Others**	**San Agustin/ Delgado**	**Worcester and the Socio-Anthro School of Hia, S.I.R.,**		**The American view of Pagkataong Pilipino**
2.		At first unrecorded, but can be culled from Filipino language, literature, stray comments by Filipinos, etc.		Ca. 1850, expression of own ideas, cf. **Hermano Pule, Burgos, Rizal,** etc. Implicit Filipino.		**Sikolohiyang Pilipino bilang Sikolohiya ng Pilipino**
C. *The Practice of Psychology by Filipinos:* 1) Normal techniques of enculturation/socialization: 2) Proto-clinical practice						
1. Enculturation/socialization. Indigenous techniques or as affected by Christianity or Islam; their survival up to our days (cf. rearing techniques; use of literature, beliefs, legends, myths, etc. for social control, etc. for the ideal personality, for example). Three stages: **Indigenous** (Ca. Pre-1300); **Modified Indigenous** (Islamic-Christian acculturative: Since Ca. 1300); **Modern Indigenous** (Americanized-commercial: Since Ca. 1900).						
2. Cf. Ancient techniques of group therapy. (poetry and alternating chants during wakes; consensus; etc.) their survivals up to the present in various Philippine contexts; tagapayo; manghuhula; use of dreams.						
IV. PSYCHO-MEDICAL SYSTEM WITH RELIGION AS COHESIVE ELEMENT AND EXPLANATION	**The Babaylan** or **Katalonan:** techniques of healing; theory of disease, its causation and therapy					

Messianic Movements → "espiritista" → Faith healing

Survival in towns and villages, overt or covert → "herbolaryo"

| 1565 | 1730 | 1900 | 1920 | 1970 |

The Western construction of history, which interprets the entire Philippines as under the dominion of some Western power or another, is readily disproved by the Tausugs of Sulu and the Maranaos of Maguindanao who maintained power and sovereignty over their territory. Exemplifying Filipino courage and bravery was Sultan Kudarat, the ruler of Cotabato, who united the natives in their fight against foreign intruders. Sultan Kudarat and his men were so successful in fighting the invaders that for 250 years the Spaniards did not return to Lanao. Hence, the Spanish dream of colonizing the entire Philippines was a total failure as attested by the intransigence of the Maranaos in the South.

Pedro Serrano Laktaw, through his lexicography, and Isabelo de los Reyes, through his works on folklore, contributed to the field of psychology of language. The area of Filipino psychopathology could be enriched by drawing from the works of Antonio Luna. The thesis of Regino Paular (1987) pioneered in the areas of history and psychopathology. We could learn more about *Juan Masipag* by examining the psychological significance of Rizal's "Sobre la Indolencia de los Filipinos" ("On the Indolence of the Filipino").

Substantial psychological insights can be culled from the works of del Pilar, who reflected on psychological topics such as love of nature (del Pilar 1888 in Panganiban and Panganiban 1954) and death (del Pilar 1907 in Panganiban and Panganiban 1954).

Before accepting the character of the Filipino as portrayed by foreigners, one must read Antonio Luna. Guthrie's (1972) view of the Filipino farmers' "subsistence motives" can be compared with the noble values and customs described in Luna's "La Tertulia Filipina" ("The Filipino Feast").

The psychological dimension of the reform movement and the revolution of 1896 have been studied in bits and pieces. The collection of myths by Mariano Ponce and *Liwanag at Dilim (Light and Darkness)* by Emilio Jacinto are valuable sources of psychological knowledge. Jacinto described the psychological distinction between *ningning* (glitter) and *liwanag* (light). Definitive studies on the writings of Apolinario Mabini, Jose Rizal and Andres Bonifacio from the psychological perspective still need to be done. The work of Almario-Velazco (1986) on the psychology of Francisco Baltazar is a start.

AMERICAN COLONIAL PSYCHOLOGY

Philippine colonial education fostered the belief that scientific psychology in the country was a Western creation, a process which supposedly started soon after Commodore George Dewey won the mock battle of Manila Bay. To begin with, undergraduate psychology courses beyond the introductory course were taught in the College of Education, University of the Philippines, using American textbooks and the English language as medium of instruction. This was less than a decade after the university itself was established in 1908 with Murray Bartlett, an American, as first president. At the time, Spanish had not altogether given way to English, literary writing in the Filipino language was on the rise, and the so-called Filipino essay ''in English'' was still a fledgling effort, a documentary proof of a struggle between the Hispanic and the indigenous in an attempt to approximate idiomatic English. As Americans gave psychology lectures in the university, the goodwill of upper and middle-class Filipinos was being won gradually by Governor-General Francis Burton Harrison's policy of attraction.

Early American Psychology Minus the Laboratory Animals

The early influence of American education and the colonial culture on Philippine psychology found concrete manifestation in the person of Agustin Alonzo. Five years of American training in advanced psychology and Harrison's policy of Filipinization paved the way for Alonzo to assume the psychology chair in the State University. To be sure, personnel indigenization annoyed the American community in the Philippines, but personnel indigenization was actually a practical policy for the Americans because it cost less to hire a Filipino. Critical positions were, of course, reserved for the American colonial administrators, but the chairmanship of the psychology department of the State University was not considered a ''critical'' position then or now. The end of Harrison's era of Filipinization in 1921 (Agoncillo 1974:28) was the beginning of American-oriented graduate psychology in the Philippines. It marked the completion of the first M.A. psychology thesis in English, written by Alonzo, at the University of the Philippines. Right after completing his M.A. requirements in 1922, Alonzo proceeded to the University of Chicago, where he received his Ph.D. in experimental psychology. It was no accident that he initially worked on a people-oriented thesis on the psychology of feeling while in Manila but shifted to the mechanistic determinism of comparative psychology in the American Midwest. In spite of Edward Lee Thorndike's influence, Alonzo somehow came through with his gentle handling of rats in a maze to provide ''manual guidance'' to his laboratory animals. Alonzo's problems and experience as an Asian in a white midwestern city impelled him to work for fellow foreign students towards the establishment of the International Center at the University of Chicago. Filipino scholars later passed through the University of Chicago's International Center and enjoyed its facilities, hardly realizing that Alonzo's efforts had led to the Center's creation. Likewise, Alonzo's pivotal role in early American colonial psychology in the Philippines passed unnoticed when he died in 1981.

Of course, neither Alonzo nor the Americans alone should be credited with the introduction of Western psychology to the Philippines. To be sure, *psicologia* was not unheard of in the Philippines at the time the U.S. Senate ratified the Treaty of Paris, thus legitimizing American annexation of the Islands. In fact, the Filipino term *sikolohiya* was derived from the Spanish *psicologia* and the term itself was already a part of the layman's vocabulary even if the spelling was standardized only much later. However, what mattered most to the "Philippine-psychology-as-an-American-creation" theorists is what they perceived as a difference in kind between Spanish rational psychology and American behavioral psychology. After all, one can credibly argue that rational psychology is a form of philosophy, and as such, appropriate in the realm of speculative thought. Similarly, the psychological treatises of Plasencia and Delgado were not meant for the *Indios*, who now call themselves Filipinos. The works of Jacinto (Santos 1935), del Pilar (1888, 1907), and Jose P. Rizal are rich sources of psychological theories and insights, but Jacinto, del Pilar and Rizal were mainly propagandists, not psychologists. Besides, it took more than two centuries from its founding in 1611 for the University of Santo Tomas to change its admissions policy to accommodate Filipinos; it was not their mission to teach Thomistic psychology to the *Indios*. And in all likelihood, the *psicologos del verbo Tagalog*, gratefully acknowledged by Emilio Aguinaldo in his inaugural speech in 1899 as president of the First Philippine Republic, were not Ph.D. (psychology) degree holders anyway. Neither were del Pilar and Jacinto. Heroes of the revolution they were, but certified psychologists they were not.

If we must demand credentials from Emilio Aguinaldo's *psicologos* then let us ask the same of William McKinley's "psychologists." Historians tell us that no less than the president of the United States of America, William McKinley, justified his venture into the Philippines on the basis of a dream and divine inspiration which spurred him to send soldiers to the Philippines to civilize and Christianize the islanders. The English language and the American system of education proved to be the most efficient instruments for the noble purpose. In fact, the first American teachers of psychology in the Philippines were not even trained in psychology. To be sure, they spoke English and administered psychological tests, but that was not enough to dislodge rational psychology, which held sway in the Philippine psychological scene at the time. The Pontifical University of Santo Tomas was not named after Thomas Aquinas for nothing. Just the same, William Howard Taft's move to impose English as the medium of instruction in the Philippines was the single master stroke which quite conveniently transferred the burden of developing psychology as a discipline in the Philippines from the hands of the Spanish-speaking friars to the shoulders of native American speakers of English. But not for long, as the colonial masters reserved the position of Director of Education for an American national as a holdout even as they intensified the pragmatic pursuit of the policy of personnel indigenization at lower levels. The American teachers of psychology in the '20s were gradually, but soon enough, replaced by a new breed of Filipino teachers. The new teachers were, unfortunately, trained in fields other than psychology, just like their American predecessors. As late as the '60s, we find instructors armed with a copy of an American textbook and a background in English literature, education, or law, handling undergraduate psychology courses. They all had one thing in common: they could lecture in reasonably good English.

The "Philippine-psychology-as-an-American-creation theory" has a sizeable number of adherents. The "theory" has no name because it is less a theory than an unchallenged assumption in the minds of American-trained Filipino psychologists. The strong version of the "theory" states that Americans brought psychology to the Philippines together with the blessings of civilization and democracy. If we are to believe this claim, then psychology as a science and profession was a "factory-sealed" importation from the West, from theory to method and application, including all the appurtenances that go with psychological practice.

McKinley's divine inspiration and "Benevolent Assimilation Proclamation" in December 1898 worked so well for psychology that even four scores later, Filipino psychologists were traveling and training in American centers of learning as Filipino Muslims travel to Mecca. A Maranao would gladly risk his life to become a *hajii*, but would a Filipino psychologist risk anything at all, much less lose his *anima*, by regularly and devoutly going to Harvard? Losing one's life is tangible; losing the "indigenous psyche" is not even easy to comprehend.

The establishment of psychology in the Philippines, according to the "straight-from-America" theory, was rather fast and easy. No resistance was met and problems were minimal. Thanks to the efficiency of the American colonial administration, it did not take too long for American-style Western psychology to take root in Philippine soil. To borrow a word from the historian Renato Constantino (1975), the "miseducation" of Filipino psychologists was rather thorough and almost complete. Not content with welcoming the Thomasites to Philippine shores, psychologists retraced the Thomasites' voyage back to North America. Indeed, Alonzo was one of the first to take such a voyage but it is to his credit that in spite of his training, he did not feel compelled to bring home to Manila, as *pasalubong*, a colony of rats and a T-maze. He shifted his research and teaching activities from experimental to educational psychology. He cannot be faulted for not directly exploiting his training. In the late '20s and early '30s, the University of the Philippines and the country had a greater need for the application of psychology to educational measurement than basic research on animal learning. It was Alonzo's energetic student, Sinforoso Padilla, who established the Experimental Psychology Laboratory at the U.P after his return from the University of Michigan in 1928. But looking back, one realizes that while Alonzo did not bring his white rats from Chicago with him, he brought something else, something truly precious to Philippine education as a handmaiden of colonial policy. Alonzo unwittingly came back from Chicago proficient in American English, with psychology as the topic of discourse. To paraphrase and modify Constantino (1975) as his ideas apply to the psychological situation:

The use of English as the medium of instruction in psychology made possible the speedy introduction of American-oriented psychology and values. With American textbooks in psychology from Thorndike, Hall, and Lindzey to Hilgard and McConnell, Filipinos began learning not only a new psychology but also a new culture. Education became miseducation because it began to de-Filipinize the Filipino psychologists, taught them to look up to American departments of psychology as always years ahead of Philippine counterparts, to regard American psychology as always superior to theirs and American society as the model par excellence for Philippine society.

Alas, the first American-trained Filipino experimental psychologist is better remembered for his classes in American-oriented educational psychology with Antonio Isidro and Sinforoso Padilla as students. Among the students of Alonzo were the young Alfredo V. Lagmay, who later served as chairman of the U.P.'s psychology department for more than two decades, and Estefania Aldaba, who got her M.A. (Psychology) in 1938 from the U.P, Ph.D. (Psychology) from the University of Michigan and much later held the highest position ever held by a psychologist in the Marcos government, that of Minister of Social Work, at the personal behest of no less than the First Lady, Madame Imelda Marcos. True enough, Philippine nationalism continues to hold its own in the face of Americanization, then as now. The initial stirrings of conflict and the manifestations of the Great Cultural Divide between the elite and the masses could not be ignored by the first generation of American-trained Filipino psychologists of the '20s. The initial entry in the cultural struggle scoreboard was one-all as Alonzo made good his long shot for a relevant Philippine educational psychology but at the same time scored for American English. It was for Manuel Carreon and Sinforoso Padilla to make follow-up attempts for the Filipino in the area of psychological measurement.

Indigenizing Psychological Tests: From Apples to Papayas

The current Philippine objection to the uncritical importation of Western psychological models is at least 60 years old. The credit for the first attempt at local psychological test development goes to Sinforoso Padilla, who authored the Philippine Mental Abilities Test. His daughter, Leila Padilla, pursued his work and interests, laying the ground for the efforts of Emeteria Lee (1973), Annadaisy Carlota (1980, 1985), Ma. Angeles Guanzon (1983, 1985a, 1985b, 1985c), and Gundelina A. Velazco (1985). However, Padilla's teaching and administrative duties kept his hands full, so to speak. It was his articulate and prolific colleague, Manuel Carreon, who took the cudgels for appropriate and relevant psychological testing. In 1926, Carreon published in New York his Ph.D. dissertation entitled *Philippine Studies in Mental Measurement*. His motivation for writing the book, his thesis, and arguments were valid, but as a faithful colonial he committed the mistake of writing in English. To think that his psychological writing could have shared the fate of its literary counterparts in the native language. Copies of the *Malaya, Ilang-Ilang,* and *Sinag-Tala* sold briskly at five centavos a copy. Not to mention the popular and durable *Liwayway*, which was available then as now in the streets of Manila, weathering the American colonial administration, a World War, the Japanese Occupation, student activism, Martial Law, the assassination of Benigno Aquino, Jr., the rise to power of Corazon Cojuangco Aquino, the murder of Lean Alejandro, and all. For his mistake Carreon paid dearly. Copies of his book were not shelved with other books on psychological testing but instead landed in the *Filipiniana* section of the university libraries in America and the Philippines. A librarian unwittingly wields a lot of power, for by classifying a book as *Filipiniana* he dooms it to limited readership. A reader of Carreon's book at the Northwestern University library rewarded Carreon's effort to communicate in English with an unsigned remark on a page margin castigating his poor mastery of the language of his colonial masters. Meanwhile, indigenous psychological testing and diagnosis flourished in remote Philippine barrios as well as right in the heart of Manila. *Pagpapatawas*, a traditional projective technique which deserves more research space than the Rorschach in Philippine psychology, was ignored and reserved as a topic for clinical psychologists and anthropologists of the future.

If Alonzo was blessed with a Governor-General Harrison and the policy of "Filipinization," Carreon was less lucky with Harrison's successor in the person of a certain Major-General Leonard Wood who believed that the Filipinos were not "prepared for independence and that it would require much more time and experience before they could prove worthy of America's trust" (Agoncillo 1974).

Perhaps Carreon was born at the wrong time with the right ideas. He should have written for *Liwayway* instead. In a manner of speaking, nobody listened to him. Educationalists and guidance counsellors went ahead and merrily administered psychological tests developed in America in a language hardly mastered by both the unsuspecting test-takers and the eager test-administrators. Some understood part of Carreon's message, modified test items to fit Philippine conditions, and got to be satisfied with what was later known as the "change-apples-to-papayas" approach to improving test validity: an approach to Philippine psychological testing which held sway from the time Hartendorp studied the correlation between breast size and the intelligence of Filipinas up to the more recent rush to test Filipino workers to certify that they are psychologically fit for work in the deserts of Saudi Arabia.

Culture works in strange ways. The Filipino banquet table no longer includes the end-of-the-year holiday apples from Wisconsin. Who cares if tropical fruits are in season? Even Chinese apples are preferred over the lowly local *atis* and *kaimito*. One might object to colonial mentality with vehemence, but who would dare match words with deeds and touch the apple in the *lechon*'s mouth? Alas, the *dalandan* (native orange) replaced the rather expensive apple. Thanks to the devaluation of the Philippine peso in response to political developments and the generosity of the World Bank, luxury fruits including apples were totally banned for a time in the Philippines. Knowing Filipino psychology, nothing is ever totally banned in the country. Even the traffic sign which says "stop" merely means "slow down and look both ways" in Manila. The *balikbayan* or returning Filipino resident from the U.S. will insist on bringing in apples even if he pays a tax on them. But woe to him who looks for the cherry on top of his *halu-halo*. The native *kaong* took the cherry's place a long time ago for the same reason apples were replaced by the local *dalandan*.

Identifying with the New Culture: From Apalachicola to Punk

American-trained Filipino psychologists, typified by Isidoro Panlasigui, who hailed from Northern Philippines and completed his Ph.D. in Educational Psychology in Iowa in 1928 through private American support, completely forgot the horrors of Balangica, Samar in the '50s and proudly identified with the "Protestant churches, schools, and colleges: the concept of democracy, the structure and practices of [American colonial] educational system and government, Baguio City and the zigzag road, the American dollar, *our* [italics added] economic and industrial system, the American sports--baseball, basketball, tennis, golf, etc" (Panlasigui 1962).

Panlasigui's admiration for Mother America showed glowingly even as he wrote about the psychology of the Filipino and as he argued for the colonial language. On the basis of a quotation from H.G. Wells, Panlasigui was quick to remind us that "the language of the conquered may be adopted by the conqueror or vice-versa." He considered it a boost to Philippine national dignity to be " culturally classified with the great natives of the Americas and Europe," and so he happily quoted Hayes ([1937] in Panlasigui 1962):

> If Europe is anything more than a geographical expres-
> sion, then the American nations--and likewise Australia and
> New Zealand and South Africa and even Serbia and the
> Philippine Islands--are, and for a long time have been, as much
> a part of Europe as British [sic], Spain, or Russia. Their
> languages are European. So are their religious beliefs, their
> social customs, their cultural traditions. Their histories are
> inextricably interwoven with Europe's.

The awesome task of Americanizing the Filipino psychologists was completed, therefore, in the person of Isidoro Panlasigui, intellectually and emotionally. But Panlasigui was not without opponents. A worthy attitudinal arch enemy was Manuel L. Quezon, who wanted a Philippine national language perhaps even at the expense of the colonial language. The most memorable quotation from Quezon is of course his fiery "I would rather have a government run like hell by Filipinos than a government run like heaven by Americans." Quezon could have his "Filipino government" so long as Panlasigui could listen to Anita Bryant's "Paper Roses," dance the American boogaloo, which replaced the Latin apalachicola, wear his *americana* (coat and tie), enjoy hotdogs and ice cream, etc. (c.f.*Colonialism in the Philippines*, Panlasigui 1962: 65-76).

Panlasigui's contribution to Philippine psychology cannot of course be found in his *Elementary Statistics, Educational Measurement and Evaluation* (1951), which amounted to nothing more than a lengthy description of how to compute the correlation coefficient, but in his more authentic *Ti Agtutubo* (19-) and *Ti Ubing* (1956).

2

THE MEETING OF EAST AND WEST

The German Roots

Psychology, as an academic discipline in the Philippines, constantly faces all sorts of problems in matters of staffing, curricular development, instructional facilities, research and publication. Considering such problems, it is indeed impressive that psychology managed to develop independently for a time at the University of San Carlos in Cebu City. San Carlos is the oldest center of learning in the Philippines, even antedating the University of Santo Tomas (U.S.T.) in Manila. The only difference is that unknown to many, U.S.T. was established as a university in 1661, ahead of San Carlos. Moghaddam's (1987) categorization of psychology in the Three Worlds would show that psychology in Cebu City has its direct roots in the Second World. However, the influence of First World psychology around the globe is not only extensive but was also entrenched much earlier in many places, including Manila. American psychology had a foothold by 1922 in the psychology departments of the U.S.T. and the University of the Philippines in the areas of experimental, educational, and counselling psychology, but psychology in the German tradition was taught for the first time much later. In 1954, a department of psychology was established at the University of San Carlos by Joseph Goertz after he spent almost 18 years of psychological work in Beijing and a couple of years in Europe before being sent to Cebu. To think that U.S. psychology has its roots in European sources as well. The medium of instruction at the University of San Carlos psychology department was and still is English while the theoretical perspective was basically German. With Goertz teaching experimental psychology in the tradition of Wundt in what has been called the ''genealogy of psychology'' in the Visayas, he was a step away from the original German edition and was using another Western language in communicating with his predominantly Cebuano-speaking students. By the time Goertz taught and used *Theoretical Psychology (After J. Lindworsky)* as a textbook (Goertz 1965), it was a wonder that the ideas of Wundt, Kulpe and Lindworsky survived. The perception experiments in the German tradition were performed semester after semester, thus tempting a Manila-based Skinnerian psychologist to refer to psychology at San Carlos as "brass and cymbals" psychology. The department of psychology at San Carlos is open to American training in psychology. Unfortunately, the people they sent to Manila or Honolulu for advanced psychology training failed to come back.

The University of San Carlos is run by the Society of the Divine Word, a Catholic religious order. However, the action in psychology in the Society is not centered in Cebu City but northeast of Cebu, in a copra-rich island called Leyte, where the Portuguese Magellan and the American MacArthur both landed. The university of interest in Leyte, aside from the U.P. at Tacloban, is Divine Word University, where the journal *Samar-Leyte Studies* comes from and where the *Pambansang Samahan sa Sikolohiyang Pilipino* or PSSP (National Association for Filipino Psychology) held its first regional conference. The output of the conference is probably a landmark in psychological publishing in the Philippines--a book entitled *Filipino Religious Psychology*--not because of the conference theme but because the title is more "sellable" than the said *Proceedings of the First Regional Conference of the Pambansang Samahan sa Sikolohiyang Pilipino.*

Tacloban, Leyte is a center of psychological activity in the Western Visayas in view of the presence of a number of colleges and universities in the area. The U.P. at Tacloban launched an undergraduate program in psychology in 1981 under the leadership of Daisy Soledad, who completed her Ph.D. (Psychology) dissertation on the Philippine Thematic Apperception Test at the U.P. in Diliman.

The Spanish Hold in España and Intramuros, Manila

Advanced training in scientific psychology has a long history at the U.S.T. With the distinction of having initiated the offering of Ph.D.-level psychology in the country, the U.S.T. not only hurdled the enormous problem of staffing for its advanced psychology program but also undertook the responsibility of providing the majority of schools in the Philippines with psychology-trained instructors. Among the pioneer psychology professors in its faculty was Jose A. Samson, the first with a Ph.D. in psychology. Emmanuel Vit Samson was a doctor of medicine while Angel de Blas was a Spanish Dominican priest and philosopher. Filipinos did not find this bothersome since the Philippines should be the last country to insist on a union-card criterion for being a psychologist, anyway. With Blas as head and founder in 1938, the U.S.T. Experimental Psychology Laboratory blazed a trail as training laboratory and published a series of workbooks, manuals, texts and exercises for student use. The department's orientation was medical and physiological. While Jose A. Samson is credited with the clinical character of the present U.S.T. psychology curriculum (Cabezon 1977), it is notable that the influence of Fr. Blas and the other Samson dominated the scene. Fondly remembered by his students, Emmanuel Vit Samson chaired the department from 1954 to 1972. He still lectures on Saturdays, on top of his responsibilities at the United Laboratories, a drug company. Angel de Blas was honored with Annual Memorial Lectures by the department and the U.S.T. Psychology Society. Meanwhile, Jose A. Samson has moved to a College in Lucena, Quezon, away from the noisy metropolis, and now actively pursues his studies on culture and personality in remote areas of the Philippines.

One might ask, what is the attitude of U.S.T. towards indigenization and the *Sikolohiyang Pilipino* perspective? Since research is needed, acceptance has been tempered with caution from the very beginning as can be gleaned from the 1977 issue of *Unitas:*

> It is regrettable that although the Rorschach and the MMPI as well as other personality tests of similar nature have been in increasing demand, no notable research has been undertaken along this line. Instead, there have been demands for local tests. Dr. J. Samson pointed out that such efforts do not exclude the construction of local tests. However, when foreign tests prove to be of high validity and reliability for the Pilipino it is better to make use of them rather than to waste efforts on devising personality inventories on questionable assumptions (Cabezon 1977: 186).

Be that as it may, the oldest university in the Far East (formerly the Colegio de Santo Rosario in 1611 and established as the University of Santo Tomas in 1616) registered another "first" by including in 1987 a subject in Filipino Psychology as an integral part of its undergraduate psychology curriculum. This was under the leadership of Dolores de Leon, who received her advanced training in clinical psychology from the U.S.T. Her clinical practice made her keenly aware of the need to study the Filipino cultural dimension in understanding the human psyche.

A national hero of the Philippines, Jose Rizal, studied at the U.S.T., where he wrote his poem "A la Juventud Filipina," which won the poetry contest sponsored by the Lyceum of Arts and Letters, U.S.T. in 1879 (del Castillo and Medina 1972, Comision Nacional de Historia 1972). Almost a hundred years hence, a Spanish priest at the same university, Padre Cavero, who was writing his psychology dissertation, when asked why he chose to be away from his homeland, answered without batting an eyelash that he was in the Philippines in 1974 "to help civilize the Filipinos." The

Spanish missionaries succeeded to a good extent. In 1986 they swiftly silenced the dissatisfaction of Filipino Dominican priests who asked too many questions and apparently wanted to wrest control of the finances of the U.S.T. away from the Spaniards, an insolence inconsistent with the sacred vow of obedience. Another school run by the Dominicans also offers training in psychology. Colegio de San Juan de Letran, founded by the Spanish Dominicans in 1630 in Intramuros, Manila, had the distinction of being the only school in Southeast Asia reportedly teaching psychology up to the mid-1970s in Spanish, a culture claimed to be similar to Filipino, psychologically speaking (Rosales 1965). The issue at Letran is not the Spanish language but the issue of authority and control. The student paper and the activities of the psychology majors are closely guarded against the intrusion of godless ideologies, a characteristic stance which made the Rev. Fr. Rector in 1958 advise graduating high school students against enrolling at the secular U.P. because the professors in that university were "devils in human form." From the Spanish era to the post-Marcos '80s, be it in the Office of the Rector at Letran or the office of the leading Philippine dignitary of the Roman Catholic Church, His Eminence Cardinal Sin, the faith must be defended and the priorities must always be clear, even if it means endorsing vigilante groups and unintended violations of human rights.

The Belgian Connection in the Cordilleras

As psychology develops in Manila and the south, a program of teaching and research is also independently developing up north in the Cordilleras. St. Louis University (S.L.U.) took the lead with Fr. Evarist Verlinden, a Belgian missionary priest, at the helm. S.L.U. as a major institution of higher learning in Northern Philippines started to offer psychology as a major field of undergraduate study in 1967. Guided by a scientific attitude, the Catholic faith and a graduate degree in psychology, Fr. Verlinden manages the Psychology Laboratory of the University. The S.L.U. Psychology Laboratory is proud of such equipment as a tachistoscope made from old camera parts but which functions even better than a first-hand apparatus. Aside from regular classroom activities, the department also provides direct experience in applied psychology through an active program in community service.

Verlinden's commitment to the contextualization of psychology into the Philippine setting faced financial constraints which made it impossible to hire an M.A.Psychology graduate from Ateneo de Manila. Instead, he had to invite fellow missionaries from Belgium with Ph.D.s in Psychology as guest professors. Curiously, the Belgians outnumber the regular local faculty in S.L.U.'s M.S. psychology program, and the teaching schedule coincides with the allowable period of time a tourist can legally stay in the country. Filipino psychology is conceptualized as mainstream Philippine psychology and not particularly oriented to the concerns of the people of the Cordillera. The course is included in the program as Psychology 228 and described as follows:

> Psychology 228 - Filipino Psychology: Philosophical Foundations and Problems: This course aims to orient the student with a broad perspective of the philosophical foundations of psychology. In particular, it defines, clarifies, analyzes, and discusses formulations of psychological theory, knowledge and methods which are developed with Philippine culture as their basis. It is concerned with the exploration of psychological constructs, such as the self-concept, the learning of prosocial behaviors, the communication process, etc., as situated specifically and given unique expression in and affected by the nuances of culture concretized in Philippine value systems, rearing and interaction patterns, and socialization styles. It presents a conceptual analysis and integration of the various theoretical data and empirical findings in a survey of selected Philippine culture-personality research material. Behavioral expressions are considered against a background of the motives and values that are institutionalized in this particular culture. Furthermore, it endeavors to strengthen the skills and competencies of the M.S. Psychology student in the areas of individual and group processes as they apply to the different areas of concern in relation to the development of the Filipino as he grows and interacts in society.

Meanwhile, the natives of the Cordilleras were reasserting their autonomy and the New People's Army was strengthening its hold on the area. Macli-ing Dulag, the leader of the Kalinga-Apayaos and Bontocs, was killed on April 24, 1980 for leading his people in the fight against the construction of the Chico River Dam. The concept of "barefoot psychologist" was broached for the first time in community psychology and field methods classes held at the foot of the mountains in Bulacan as psychology and anthropology students from lowland universities climbed up north to the Cordilleras. Macli-ing was not alone.

American Legacy at Diliman and Manila's University Belt

With a background in philosophy from a department steeped in logical positivism and staunchly against the sectarianism foisted by the Catholics through the then-powerful University of the Philippines Student Catholic Action (UPSCA), Alfredo V. Lagmay from U.P. Diliman was sent to the United States ostensibly on a fellowship precisely to weaken the U.P. Department of Philosophy, led by an articulate, charismatic and controversial agnostic-philosopher, Ricardo Pascual. Lagmay's colleagues in the department were also sent abroad, not to strengthen the Philosophy Department but to neutralize it. Ruben Santos-Cuyugan was sent to study sociology; Jose Encarnacion, Jr. economics; and Alfredo V. Lagmay, psychology at Harvard, where he trained with B.F.Skinner in experimental psychology.

Lagmay came back to the U.P. with a Ph.D. in psychology from Harvard in 1955. The U.P. Department of Psychology was then administratively a part of the College of Education. Lagmay's first move was to transfer the department to the College of Liberal Arts, re-orienting psychology's applied educational perspective at the U.P. to a basic scientific orientation.

A year earlier and for about the same number of years, Emmanuel Vit Samson chaired the U.S.T. psychology department (1954-1972), while Lagmay chaired the U.P. psychology department (1955-1976). They both witnessed historical developments, from the American-inspired Magsaysay campaign to pacify the *Hukbalahap* to the resurgence of nationalism under the leadership of Claro M. Recto, from President Carlos Garcia's Filipino First policy and President Diosdado Macapagal's MAPHILINDO (a Southeast Asian regionalism which antedates ASEAN) to President Ferdinand Marcos' declaration of Martial Law. Lagmay pushed for experimental psychology at a time colleagues at the State University were raising eyebrows at the mere mention of a science-oriented psychology. Experimental psychology is now an integral part of the undergraduate psychology curricula in Philippine schools but Lagmay did not quite succeed in promoting behavior analysis in the Skinnerian tradition. Even to date, the said course is not offered in a good number of Philippine colleges and universities. Just the same, Lagmay is better known as a "Skinnerian." It did not matter if he was also deeply influenced by Carl Rogers; the U.P.Department of Psychology was perceived as behavioral in orientation from the late '50s to the early '70s. Ironically, the U.S.T. was seen as psychoanalytic in orientation, together with the unjustified verdict that to be psychoanalytic is "unscientific."

Lagmay's students included Angelina Ramirez, who chaired the U.S.T. psychology department in the mid-'70s; Abraham Felipe, who studied the psychology of popular Tagalog short stories before proceeding to Yale for his Ph.D. in social psychology, later assuming the concurrent positions of president of the Fund for Assistance to Private Education (FAPE) and Deputy Minister of Education (the second highest position a psychologist held under the Marcos government); and Robert Lawless, who wrote a critical review of personality and culture studies in the Philippines.

In another campus, also within the Roman Catholic dominion, at a school run by American Jesuits before the war, another battle had to be fought in the early '60s, perhaps not different in kind but definitely different in character. From the very beginning it was a lonely fight at the Ateneo de Manila, but Jaime Bulatao, a clinical psychologist and Jesuit priest who returned from Fordham University in 1961 and established the psychology department at the Ateneo, taught Sigmund Freud, against the wishes of his own dean. The dean felt so strongly against Freud, saying that he would allow the teaching of Freudian Psychology "only over his dead body." Dissociating Freud's teachings from the horrors of sex and immorality was the first item in Bulatao's psychology agenda. Fortunately, taking Freud's side cannot be all that bad in a culture where *libido* has an alliterative counterpart in *libog,* a word which always makes the Filipino smile. The local mind accepts sex as an indigenous birthright in the first place.

To fight for sex is one thing but to fight for money is another. Bulatao's bigger problem was the survival of the psychology department at the Ateneo de Manila when the Ateneo was still a college. Psychology had to be applied if business and industry were to support it. Thus, an industrial psychology program was evolved. Bulatao and the Ateneo psychology department's passion, however, is not industrial psychology but clinical psychology, using publications as index. But then again, it is no easy task to draw the line between scientific clinical psychology and spiritual solace from one's religious faith. Bulatao succeeded in integrating the two by allowing his calendar to include anything from therapy sessions to the "exorcism" of evil spirits lodged in a body, a house, or any other abode. Nothing as dramatic as William Peter Blatty's *Exorcist* or Steven Spielberg's *Poltergeist* but certainly reassuring to people who want their house or office blessed before they move in. After all, what is psychotherapy if not the exorcism of a disturbed psyche? Besides, Western psychiatric terminology does not communicate effectively to the local mind. Bulatao's contribution to indigenous psychology lies not in his crystal balls and dousing rods but in his insightful appreciation of the *albularyo* (local healer) even as he documents their psychology in the language of hypnotherapy and altered states of consciousness.

Nonetheless, Philippine psychology from Alonzo to Bulatao would be healthier if Filipinos looked at centers of learning besides the United States as sources of psychological skills and knowledge. Even if we limit psychology to the English-speaking world, one immediately notices that Americans lord it over the Philippines. The *Philippine Journal of Psychology* hardly ever includes any articles with references to non-American English-language journals. Australia, New Zealand, Canada and England might as well disappear from the psychological map. It wouldn't make a difference to psychology in the Philippines. Even Philippine references started to appear only in the middle '70s.

The emergence of Japan as an Asian economic power was not altogether irrelevant to the enviable "approach-approach" conflict faced by del Pilar in choosing between a Mombushu and a Fulbright. However, the American-oriented pattern established in two generations cannot be changed overnight. General Gregorio del Pilar's grandnephew and namesake "chose" to go to Washington D.C. Similarly, the heavy hand, or call it "informed judgement," of the National Intelligence and Security

Agency of the Marcos government prevented the departure of Danilo Tuazon for Moscow for advanced training in physiological psychology. A Russian scholarship was not enough. Moscow must wait. Aside from the language and culture barriers which Tuazon agreed to hurdle, a political barrier to the development of Philippine psychology proved to be formidable. Assurances of getting a Russian visa were useless without a Philippine exit permit. The fear of repatriating an undesirable ideology outweighed the possibility of "smuggling a bible across Russian immigration authorities." As luck would have it, Tuazon learned Japanese and went to Keio University instead. The first dissertation on the area of perceptual psychology written in Filipino was based on experiments done in a Japanese laboratory from 1987-1990 by Danilo Bv. Tuazon.

Locally trained psychologists are not wanting in role models. A foremost Filipino educator, Paz Policarpio-Mendez developed Ph.D.-level courses in psychology at the Centro Escolar University, including a course on Filipino Personality and another on Contemporary Sources of Philippine Psychology which were taught in Filipino. Centro Escolar University has the distinction of having published in 1983 *Punimulang Sikolohiya*, the first psychology textbook incorporating Philippine research materials and using the Filipino language. The book was prepared by the Department of Behavioral Sciences, Centro Escolar University, and rendered in Filipino by Cecilia G. Valmonte. The use of Filipino was not altogether easy. Various approaches to the language can confuse the uninitiated. Gonzalo del Rosario, for one, advocated the development and use of the national language in science and technology, although one almost has to enroll in his class to understand his Filipino. His influence was felt at the National Science Development Board (NSDB) Committee on Technical Terminology. For example, the NSDB committee's Filipino term for the word psychology, is *dalub-isipan* (expertise-mind). A psychologist is a *dalub-isip* (expert-mind). Mental is *isipan*. Ideation is *isaisip*. Intellectual is *isipnon* when used as a noun but *pang-isipan* or *maka-isipnon* when used as an adjective. Stimulus is *ganyak*. Response is *tugon*. Reflex is *balikusa*. Statistic is *himalak*. And so on (Lupon sa Agham, NSDB 1970).

Scrupulous purism in language can be a problem in a country trying to catch up with fast moving technological changes. But the primary problem as seen by the government of Corazon Aquino is neither language nor culture nor the separation of church and state but "economic recovery." The economic problem is not articulated in terms of a Great Cultural Divide separating the rich and the poor but said separation is indeed a major problem in Philippine psychology, if not in the rest of the Third World. The spiritual dimension of economic segregation goes as far as differentiating the benevolent "God of the rich" from the powerful but distant "God of the poor" (Mataragnon 1984). Not only do the poor eat different food, if they eat at all, but they also have their own tastes in leisure and entertainment. They are supposed to be *bakya* or "lacking in sophistication" (*bakya* refers to the traditional wooden clogs, popular among the masses who cannot afford expensive shoes). In fact, they have their own culture and speak their own language. While the elite speak English and occasionally throw in some French for comfort, the Filipino masses speak Filipino and a regional language. If they happen to speak Kiniray-a or Itawis instead of Hiligaynon or Ivatan, they might feel ashamed of their own language, an affliction they share with Tagalogs who are comfortable with the thought that they don't understand Tagalog.

In psychological training, elitism and the Great Cultural Divide manifest themselves even in one's "choice" of school. Manuel L. Quezon University's psychology program was a brainchild and practically the life work of an esteemed psychologist in the person of Agustin Alonzo. However, MLQU is a school for the working class. MLQU students don't speak English with an accent characteristic of students from elite schools but they speak good Filipino. In fact, their Filipino program is way ahead of the others, judging from the quality and number of theses submitted in Filipino to the MLQU Graduate School. It is true that "part-time" students also enroll at elite schools such as De La Salle and Ateneo but they invariably work in multinational corporations or hold otherwise stable jobs. Let the rich get quality education from a school for the rich. Nothing absolutely wrong with that but separating the haves from the have-nots can be vicious if an MLQU graduate cannot get a teaching job at De La Salle, for example. Economic mobility in a democracy, Philippine style, can be a long and painful process. The National College Entrance Examination has a built-in bias for the English-speaking elite but the Filipino-speaking natives also value a university education even if in the final analysis, all they have is a passport to a job as construction worker in the Middle East or as a domestic in Hong Kong. Or they can get a scholarship at De La Salle's Ph.D. counselling psychology program and wait a while until they become bona fide graduates of a school for the gentry.

3

TOWARDS A
LIBERATION PSYCHOLOGY

Sikolohiyang Pilipino:
A New Consciousness in Philippine Psychology

Given the colonial background of Philippine psychology, and considering the Great Cultural Divide as East meets West in the development of psychological thought in the Philippines, a psychology movement has evolved in the country emphasizing (1) identity and national consciousness, specifically looking at the social sciences as the study of man and *diwa* (consciousness and meaning), or the indigenous conception and definition of the psyche, as a focus of social psychological research; (2) social awareness and involvement as dictated by an objective analysis of social issues and problems, (3) national and ethnic cultures and languages, including the study of early or traditional psychology called *kinagisnang sikolohiya* by Salazar (1983); and (4) bases and application of indigenous psychology in health practices, agriculture, art, mass media, religion, etc. but also including the psychology of behavior and human abilities as demonstrated in Western psychology and found applicable to the Philippine setting.

The movement, often referred to as *sikolohiyang Pilipino*, has been considered by many psychologists and social scientists as a positive step in the development of psychology in the country. Finally, with the advent of *sikolohiyang Pilipino*, there is less reliance on Western models in the study of psychology as it urges Filipino psychologists to analyze and confront social problems, not from a Western perspective, but from the indigenous Filipino viewpoint.

Problems beset Philippine society: Government troops on the alert against military mutineers.

The massive influence of the United States in all spheres of Filipino life predisposes the Filipino to adopt the colonial viewpoint

Sikolohiyang Pilipino is the embodiment of the systematic and scientific study, appreciation and application of indigenous knowledge for, of and by the Filipinos of their own psychological make-up, society and culture, rooted in their historical past, ethnic diversity and the dynamic interaction of Filipinos with forces within and outside their social and physical boundaries. Since its institution in the early 1970's, it has developed as a distinct field in Philippine social science and has, in fact, largely set the trend insofar as the future of indigenous social science is concerned.

Sikolohiyang Pilipino traces its roots to liberalism, the propaganda movement, the writings of Jacinto, Mabini and del Pilar which were all imbued with nationalistic fervor. This has elicited diverse reactions from different groups. On the one hand, it has been questioned as rather "nativistic" in orientation for its inordinate attachment to tradition and allegedly backward practices of indigenous cultural communities. On the other hand, *sikolohiyang Pilipino* has been branded by avid adherents of Western social science models and approaches as rather radical in orientation for challenging establishment psychology.

Both views, however, are inaccurate. *Sikolohiyang Pilipino* only seeks to put things in their proper perspective and check the imbalance resulting from extreme reliance on Western models as a basis for analyzing Philippine social realities. *Sikolohiyang Pilipino* merely attempts to find application and bases of Filipino psychology in indigenous health practices, agriculture, art, religion and a people-oriented mass media. Through this, *sikolohiyang Pilipino* seeks to explain Philippine realities from the Filipino perspective, taking into account the peculiarities and distinct values and characteristics of the Filipino which the Western models invariably fail to explain or consider.

Sikolohiyang Pilipino gathers data on the Filipino psyche by utilizing culturally appropriate field methods in the form of *pagtatanong-tanong* ("asking around"), *pakikiramdam* ("shared inner perception"), *panunuluyan* ("staying with"), and *pakikipamuhay* ("living with"), among others. This is in contrast to dominant methods of data gathering which fail to take into account the cultural characteristics of the Filipino, thus rendering the findings of such research questionable.

As such, *sikolohiyang Pilipino* has three primary areas of protest as it argues against a psychology which fosters colonialism and its attendant characteristics among the Filipino people. First, as a *sikolohiyang malaya* ("liberated psychology"), it is against a psychology which perpetuates the colonial status of the Filipino mind. The psychology of *pagbabagong-isip* ("reawakening") is seen as a step towards the decolonization of the Filipino psyche leading to the development of national consciousness.

Second, *sikolohiyang Pilipino* fights against the imposition in a Third World country like the Philippines of psychologies developed in and found appropriate only to industrialized countries, such that *sikolohiyang pang-industriya* ("industrial psychology"), is reconceptualized as an aspect of *sikolohiyang pangkabuhayan* ("livelihood/economic psychology"). Consequently, there is a shift in theoretical and research focus leading to a change in the application of psychology towards serving the underserved. This, in turn, means a return of the psychologist from the city to the rural village.

Third, *sikolohiyang Pilipino* as a *sikolohiyang mapagpalaya* ("liberating psychology") denounces an elite-oriented psychology used for the exploitation of the masses.

In terms of psychological practice, *sikolohiyang Pilipino* draws from folk practices and indigenous techniques such as the *babaylan* or *catalonan* (also spelled *katalonan*) techniques of healing. It also identifies and utilizes concepts and methods from local religio-political movements. *Sikolohiyang Pilipino* as *sikolohiyang pangnayon* ("community/rural psychology) moves the scholar to return to the village to learn from them with the aim of later serving them by making use of what he has learned. As such, *sikolohiyang Pilipino* is a call for social action.

As far as its position on the science-humanism issue is concerned, *sikolohiyang Pilipino* refuses to concede that the differences in the orientation of science and humanism are irreconcilable. *Sikolohiyang Pilipino* utilizes scientific methodology in the study of psychological phenomena. However, it goes beyond the cold and impartial methods employed by science in the belief that science is only a means to a more fundamental end which is to serve the welfare of man, including the Filipino. *Sikolohiyang Pilipino* is concerned not only with the universal validity of psychological science but also in utilizing such for the purpose of serving the interest of all mankind, thereby affording protection to disadvantaged Third World countries like the Philippines. *Sikolohiyang Pilipino* thus aims to use science to enhance, not to dehumanize, man.

From the viewpoint of *sikolohiyang Pilipino*, the scientific and humanistic approaches are both valid as *sikolohiyang Pilipino* seeks to develop psychology not only as a science but also as an art. The Filipino psychologist should be able to utilize psychology as an art not by mechanically applying scientific findings but by creatively adopting them to varying circumstances regardless of the state of scientific knowledge at the time.

One can therefore look for the universal that can emanate from cross-indigenous methods and theories but this does not mean that one has to set aside and ignore the specific aspects of man associated with his culture. As *sikolohiyang Pilipino* recognizes the demands of universal science, it likewise appreciates the value of affirming the peculiarity and distinctness of man as a socio-cultural being.

Sikolohiyang Pilipino emphasizes not only the objective study of psychology but also the use of the science of psychology as a tool in developing a Philippine national culture. This move should correct the imbalance brought about by a Western-dominated psychology which is inimical to the aspirations of the Filipino.

Sikolohiyang Pilipino uses both phenomenological and behavioristic concepts.

But unlike its Western counterpart, which gives emphasis to individual experience, it puts greater weight on the collective experience of a people with a common bond of history. *Sikolohiyang Pilipino* also attaches greater importance to *kamalayan* (psyche) which can be shared by an entire nation, giving only subsidiary importance to *ulirat* (lower level of individual, physical consciousness).

Further, *sikolohiyang Pilipino* methodologically leans on the side of analysis but interprets the result of analysis with a bias for wholeness. In analyzing the results of a social science study, for instance, it relies not only on the scientific analysis of the findings but also takes into account in its interpretation other equally, if not even more, important variables like the historical background, social context, political implications and cultural meaning of the study.

Sikolohiyang Pilipino is therefore a liberation psychology which seeks to establish a truly universal psychology in the service of all mankind but with special emphasis on the Filipino. In this sense, *sikolohiyang Pilipino* seeks to promote a new consciousness with the Filipino taking center stage. Table II outlines the major characteristics of *sikolohiyang Pilipino* as an indigenous Asian psychology.

The new consciousness, labelled *sikolohiyang Pilipino* reflecting Filipino psychological knowledge, has emerged through the use of the local language as a tool for the identification and rediscovery of indigenous concepts and as an appropriate medium for the delineation and articulation of Philippine realities together with the development of a scientific literature which embodies the psychology of the Filipino people. For a start, the Filipino language itself provides the basis for proposing *sikolohiyang Pilipino* as the study of *diwa* (psyche), which directly refers to the wealth of ideas implied by the philosophical concept of "essence" and an entire range of psychological concepts from awareness to motives to behavior.

Sikolohiyang Pilipino can be explained through a metaphor: a characteristic way of clarifying concepts in the Asian manner. For example, emphasis should be given to the difference between a "person in the house" (*tao sa bahay*) and a "house person" (*taong-bahay*). A "person in the house" may be someone who just passed by, a visitor who is not voluntarily or necessarily interested in staying there. But a "house person" (*taong-bahay*) has a role and a meaning in that house, so he is there. *Sikolohiyang Pilipino* is like a "house person" as it focuses on indigenous developments in the field of psychology from the Filipino perspective. It is most commonly understood to mean the psychology of the Filipino--his character, his values and his *paninindigan* or principles. But more importantly, *sikolohiyang Pilipino* precisely refers to psychological theory, knowledge, method and application developed with the Filipino culture as basis (Enriquez 1974).

Ventura (1980) summarizes this orientation thus:

TABLE II
Major Characteristics of *Sikolohiyang Pilipino*
as an Indigenous Asian Psychology*

Philosophical antecedents

Empirical philosophy, academic-scientific psychology, the ideas and teachings of Ricardo Pascual,
logical analysis of language.
Rational philosophy, the clerical tradition, phenomenology, Thomistic philosophy and psychology.
Liberalism, the propaganda movement, the writings of Jacinto, Mabini and del Pilar, ethnic psychology.

Principal emphasis in psychology

Identity and national consciousness
Social awareness and involvement
Psychology of language and culture
Applications and bases of Filipino psychology in health practices, agriculture, art, mass media,
religion, etc.

Principal methods of investigation

Cross-indigenous method
Multi-method multi-language, laboratory, psychometric, etc.
Appropriate field methods: *pagtatanong-tanong, pakikiramdam, panunuluyan, pakikipamuhay,* etc.
Total approach: "triangulation method"

Primary areas of protest

Against a psychology that perpetuates the colonial status of the Filipino mind
Against a psychology used for the exploitation of the masses
Against the imposition to a Third World country of psychologies developed in industrialized countries

Position on psychological practice

Conceptualization of psychological practice in a Philippine context (Sikolohiyang
Pang-industriya vs. *Pangkabuhayan*, Sikolohiyang *Pangklinika* vs. *Pangkalusugan*).
Concerned with folk practices/indigenous techniques, *babaylan,* or *katalonan* techniques
of healing. Popular religio-political movements. Community/rural psychology
(*aksyong panlipunan*, Bulacan Community Field Station).

Position on science-humanism issue

Concerned with both. Scientific and humanistic approaches are both valid.
Develops psychology as a science and psychology as an art.

Position on mentalism-behaviorism issue

Admitted both but with lesser emphasis on individual experience and with greater emphasis
on the collective experience of a people with a common bond of history.
Greater importance attached to *kamalayan* (psyche), thus, subsidiary importance
attached to *ulirat* (lower level of physical consciousness).

Position on analysis-wholeness issue

Not a big issue. Methodologically on the side of analysis but interprets the result of analysis
with a bias for wholeness.

---

*As culled from Pe-Pua's *Sikolohiyang Pilipino: Teorya, Metodo at Gamit* (1982), San Buenaventura's
Pilosopikal na Batayan ng Sikolohiyang Pilipino (1983), Salazar's *Ethnic Psychology and History* (1983),
Lagmay's *Western Psychology in the Philippines: Impact and Response* (1984), and publications of the *Pambansang
Samahan at Sikolohiyang Pilipino* and the Philippine Psychology Research and Training House.

A reader of Philippine psychology literature will immediately note that the decade of the '70s was marked by a concern for indigenization--a recognition of language as a basic variable in personality, social psychology and testing; a broadening of the data base of Filipino psychology through a concern for studying individuals in their natural social setting; rediscovering ties between Filipino psychology and other fields of study; and greater involvement, on a nationwide level, of Filipino social scientists in the development of the literature of Filipino psychology. In the University of the Philippines, the interest in indigenization brought about research on Philippine psycholinguistics, Filipino concepts and cognition, and master's theses which utilized language as a major variable (Ventura 1973, Lazo 1974, Alfonso 1974). Along with this recognition of the importance of language came a consciousness of the limitations, and sometimes emptiness, of Western theories and methods. Students became more critical about the Western orientation in research and in the classroom. Mangulabnan (1977) referred to this as *"metodong angat-patong"* (literally, "lift-pile" method) and aptly described the uncritical acceptance and use of Western theories and strategies.

Sikolohiyang Pilipino does not advocate the discarding of foreign theories of behavior on the ground of origin. Uncritical rejection is just as dangerous as uncritical acceptance of Western theories. More accurately, *sikolohiyang Pilipino* is a call for the exercise of care in the adoption of foreign theories. Bonifacio (1980) explains:

> [We have to] exercise care in using them [Western theories] because the actual sources of such explanations are very different from ours. While it is true that no one in any society is exempt from psychological problems, we have to underscore the fact that the sources of such problems differ greatly from one society to another. For instance, the sources of deprivation of a Western man are different from that of an Asian [in the Third World]. In both societies, deprivation is experienced but it would be safe to conclude that since the Asian [in the Third World] has less access to material resources, his tolerance threshold will be higher.

Sociopolitical Problems, Ethnic Diversity and Neo-Colonialism

Sikolohiyang Pilipino, as a perspective, urges the Filipino psychologist to confront social problems and national issues as part of his responsibility. Cipres-Ortega (1980) reported a ferment in its earliest stage of development. Issues considered in *sikolohiyang Pilipino*'s incipient stage include the question of what language to use in psychological research, teaching, and publication: Pilipino or Filipino. Choosing between P and F becomes trivial, once the language issue gets to be resolved as a matter of choosing between a multilanguage-based 28-letter alphabet and a Tagalog-based 20-letter *abakada*. Such a choice is definitely simpler than choosing between a colonial and an indigenous language.

The language issue stirred nationalistic sentiments in Manila's college corridors and triggered feverish debates in the 1971 Constitutional Convention. Fifteen years later, Filipino was unanimously proclaimed the national language of the Philippines by the Constitutional Commission of 1986. Although the Filipino people ratified the 1987 Constitution, English remained the primary language of education used by psychology teachers in the American-oriented system of Philippine education.

Meanwhile, the national *lingua franca* continues to be forged "obstinately" by the man-on-the-street in his day-to-day transactions. Even the medium of television which used to be the preserve of the English-speaking elite had to give way to the language of the people. For the Filipino social scientist, the choice after all was not between a P and an F but between the language of the man-on-the-street and a colonial language. *Sikolohiyang Pilipino* chose what Sicat (1976) called the "living Filipino language."

A second concern also reported by Cipres-Ortega (1980) has to do with the delineation of the "Filipino" in Filipino psychology. "Filipino" may refer to the mainstream urbanized *Manileño* or the "unsophisticated" *provinciano*. The word "Filipino" conjures the image of one who belongs to a major ethnic group but one from a minority group is just as Filipino. Samson (1965) therefore referred to "psychologies" of Filipinos because of the cultural and ethnic diversity of the Filipino people.

The issue of ethnic diversity may seem primarily political but its implication as a basis for the development of psychological theory and research cannot be overlooked. After all, reference to cultural distinctions within the Filipino society does not imply a fragmented Philippine society. Rather, the distinctions in the culture(s) of the people provide a challenge to psychological research and a rich base for a truly national culture. The theme of the sixth annual *Pambansang Samahan sa Sikolohiyang Pilipino* convention held in Legaspi, Albay was precisely the contributions of ethnic consciousness to Filipino psychology.

Looking at ethnic diversity as a resource makes sense in a psychology which gives greater emphasis to the collective experiences of a people with a common bond of history.

While excitement regarding language and cultural heterogeneity may bring to the fore volatile sociopolitical problems, the concern for professionalization, social problems, and universality has brought about issues which stirred professional and academic circles at the campuses of Loyola Heights and Diliman. A genuine concern for professional growth and commitment to psychology as a discipline fostered unity despite attitudinal and theoretical differences. Licuanan (1979) urged Filipino psychologists to be more involved in the social and political problems of the country. She asked:

> Is it because we don't take strong stands? But we do! We do feel very strongly about certain things. At our conventions, in the classroom, in our writing and even in foreign meetings we take strong positions and call each other names such as "Western-oriented psychologists" or "behaviorists." Always of course within the bounds of *pakikipagkapwa-tao* or is it *pakikisama?* We have feuds between behaviorists and humanists that have spanned generations. We have issues such as indigenous vs. western, scientific rigor vs. *kapa-kapa*, verbal vs. nonverbal tests. Yes, we do take strong stands but perhaps our passion is wasted on each other. We have our in-house battles while outside, the Philippines wages a war against poverty, against underdevelopment, against the many problems of education, housing, graft and corruption, multinational corporations, population, etc....

It takes a Socrates to choose a human being dissatisfied over a beast satisfied, but must the Filipino contend with a borrowed consciousness in exchange for a full meal? While recognizing *sikolohiyang Pilipino* as an attempt at conceptual and methodological improvement, Licuanan's test of psychology's worth as a discipline somehow manages to exclude an appreciation of the link between colonization and poverty. A decolonized psychology can inspire but who needs inspiration on an empty stomach? She explained further:

> I do not mean to undervalue our attempts at developing psychological theories and at improving our methodology. These are vitally necessary for our survival as a discipline. But I do believe very strongly that our true worth as a discipline lies in how we are able to help solve the problems of our country today. I am sincere when I say that the concept of *kapwa* is very exciting and even inspiring. But how I wish...*kapwa* could feed all the hungry Filipinos, house them and give them the education they deserve (Licuanan 1979).

Philippine psychology's colonial character as a captive of an American-oriented, English-speaking world is one of *sikolohiyang Pilipino*'s major areas of protest. Psychology as a Western-oriented discipline is supposed to be partial to universal findings, to "generalizability" and external validity. The scientific character of psychology is accepted by *sikolohiyang Pilipino* but its universality is questioned by the Filipino as it is being questioned elsewhere (e.g., in Mexico by Rogelio Diaz-Guerrero, 1977). The history of psychology as it has evolved in the Western tradition can be interpreted as moving towards the goal of a truly global psychology. Unfortunately, psychology is still far from that goal in spite of over a hundred years of scientific research reckoned from the time Wilhelm Wundt established a laboratory of psychology in Leipzig, Germany in 1879.

Cultural Revalidation and Theoretical Reorientation

Regardless of differing theoretical persuasions, Filipino psychologists generally recognize the importance of cultural validation. Only the eager exponents of the "latest" theories and approaches gathered from short-term visits to Boston, Chicago or Los Angeles would immediately apply their newly acquired techniques without bothering with the problems of adaptation. Respect for cultural validation was slow in coming for many of what Bulatao alliteratively identified as "pious pupils of Piaget," daring disciples of Drucker" and "fervent followers of Freud." Even the "scientific students of Skinner" had to be chided:

> At present, the typical psychology department in the Third World sports a collection of psychology books and journals, ninety-five percent of which comes from the Western world. Since the behavioral research they contain has been mostly on Western subjects, there rises an obligation to put a sign that reads something like this: "The Philippine Minister of Education and Culture has certified that the behavioral conclusions of these articles are true of the American population but not necessarily true for Filipinos. Readers should beware for their "intellectual health." Of course, the scientific students of Skinner have one advantage. Being much devoted to the laboratory, they are more familiar with experimental data than their book-bound brothers. Furthermore, [locally-raised] pigeons differ less from American pigeons than their human counterparts, (we supposed). But is it not possible now further to declare their independence from the interests and instrumentation of the United States? Having once learned scientific methodology, should they not now apply this methodology and

create instruments to answer questions that face a developing
nation, such as to formulate learning strategies suited to the
Filipino or to stabilizing behavior therapy workable at the out-
patient clinic of the Philippine General Hospital? (Bulatao
1979a).

Sikolohiyang Pilipino as an optional subject was instituted and offered for the
first time at the undergraduate level at the University of the Philippines in 1978. At
home with a new consciousness, Jose Ma. Bartolome, who first taught the course, was
painfully aware of the slow pace of theoretical reorientation especially with a class of
undergraduate juniors and seniors who enrolled in the course as an elective, hoping to
find a teacher ready to deliver a dissertation on the psychology, values, and behavior
of the Filipino. They later found that the course was meant for psychology majors who
must be shown the scope and limits of a psychology based on Filipino culture and
experience.The problem of theoretical reorientation as reported by Atal(1979) had to
be sorted out by Bartolome and his colleagues at the U.P.Department of Political
Science and St. Scholastica's College:

While there is too much iconoclastic talk about the
domination of alien models and theories and their inappropriateness, there is very little to commend as respectable replace-
ments. Along with severe criticism of the so-called "capital-
ist," "status quoist," "western," "American" social science, we may come across writings that very enthusiastically
prescribe "Marxism" as an alternative. Efforts are still needed
to test the proclaimed universality of established theories and
models in a variety of settings. It is not so much a replacement
that is really needed if one wants to pursue the goal of a
universal science--and not of setting up "schools of thought,"
like sects creating a priesthood and a blind following. Such
genuine efforts that go beyond reactive rhapsodies are rare to
find (Atal 1979).

Atal recognized that some efforts are being made, by citing as an example the
work of Pakistani economist Mahbub Ul Haq, who reconsidered basic premises of a
development paradigm learned at Harvard and Yale, thus allowing a reformulation of
strategy. Unresolved theoretical issues did not deter Bartolome's students from
integrating research studies on Filipino psychology even if it meant including Ateneo-
IPC studies viewed as the "latest avatar of the foreign or external view of the
psychology of Filipinos" by Salazar (1983) and as "American" social science by
David (1977) and others. Explaining the theoretical bases of one's methodology and

practice is very important and corollary to the task of "weaning *sikolohiyang Pilipino* from its colonial mooring." In addition, the excitement of rediscovery motivated the identification and development of culturally relevant psychological concepts such as *kapwa* (shared identity) and *pakiramdam* (shared inner perception) (Enriquez 1978, Mataragnon 1983). The same standards of scientific validity apply to the indigenous world-view, therefore the need to scientifically revalidate culturally accepted and time-tested local concepts and methods such as *pagtatanung-tanong* (Pe-Pua 1985).

An Alternative Psychology Literature in Filipino

Armed with a history of personal involvement in the development of the theoretical underpinnings of *Sikolohiyang Pilipino* and with the confidence of one who had concrete experience with the actual application of indigenous methods, Rogelia Pe-Pua took over where Bartolome left off. Pe-Pua (1982) faced the problems of articulating the concepts and methods of Filipino psychology head-on with a book entitled *Sikolohiyang Pilipino: Teorya, Metodo at Gamit (Filipino Psychology: Theory, Method and Application).* For the first time, a compilation of papers on Filipino psychology was made available for student use. The compilation is in English and Filipino, reflecting the language situation in the Philippine academic setting. Actually, English is still dominant in the classroom and the conference halls of the Philippine Social Science Council but Filipino has definitely emerged as a language of the educated Filipino of the '70s. The indecision lies not in what language to use but in how much linguistic borrowing from English should be tolerated or encouraged. Ernesto Constantino, a renowned linguist, vehemently argues against purism, allowing Filipino psychologists to sleep soundly even after using such words as *"reimpors"* (reinforce) in written reports and *"saykayatri"* (psychiatry) in oral presentations.

With Pe-Pua's anthology, *sikolohiyang Pilipino* as a theoretical perspective has finally come to print in textbook form instead of coming out in isolated mimeographed articles, thus satisfying form-oriented scholars who have assumed values appropriate to First World conditions. In their thinking, the availability of printed books suggests there might be basis for the indigenous psychology movement. The form of articulation is not a measure of validity but the mystique of the printed word, especially if "in English and imported from the United States" still enthralls the captive Filipino psychologist.

The growth of the *sikolohiyang Pilipino* literature in the '80s gives one the feeling that the Filipino language is making up for lost time in the discipline of psychology. Barely three years after the publication of Pe-Pua's book, another anthology of Filipino psychology articles came out under the joint editorship of a secular priest-anthropologist and a nun: Fr. Allen Aganon and Sr. Ma. Assumpta David, RVM (1985). The compilation entitled *Sikolohiyang Pilipino: Isyu, Pananaw at Kaalaman* is in many ways a sequel to Pe-Pua's book. It is aptly subtitled *New*

Directions in Indigenous Psychology. Considering the cost of publication in an economically deprived country, an anthology every three years aside from annual publications is frequent indeed.

Within the same period, non-Tagalogs wrote their theses in the Filipino language, disputing the mistaken belief that Filipino is the preserve of Tagalogs. Mario San Buenaventura, a native speaker of the Bikolnon language of Oas, Albay, wrote his thesis on the "Philosophical Basis of *Sikolohiyang Pilipino*" in the Filipino language ("*Mga Batayang Pilosopikal ng Sikolohiyang Pilipino*") in 1983. Another non-Tagalog, Patricia de Peralta, a native of Laoag, Ilocos Norte, contributed to the literature of *Sikolohiyang Pilipino* in the Filipino language on the topic of Ilokano folk stories. Ma. Angeles Guanzon's thesis on the "*Panukat ng Ugali at Pagkatao*" was also written in Filipino: Ma. Angeles Guanzon is Bikolana. Edilberto Tiempo's (Gonzalez and Bautista 1981) idea of a "fourth colonization" of the Filipinos, which reminded Bonifacio Sibayan, *Kasaping Pandangal* (honorary member) of the *Pambansang Samahan sa Sikolohiyang Pilipino*, of Salvador de Madariaga's solipsistic anguish over "the most difficult kind of colonization" which is none other than "colonization by one's own people," should end as an unfounded fear and as highly inappropriate, insofar as *sikolohiyang Pilipino* is concerned.

The philosophical position of *sikolohiyang Pilipino* turns the problem of regionalism and language diversity in the Philippines into an advantage. Ethnic diversity and ethnic consciousness enrich national culture and help define the Filipino psyche. It is perhaps a happy coincidence that the majority of the contributors to the *sikolohiyang Pilipino* literature are in fact non-Tagalogs. The same observation holds true for psychologists who pioneered in the teaching of psychology in Filipino. Marylou Onglatco lectured in Filipino despite her Chinese accent. Proud of their Chinese heritage but definitely loyal to their adopted homeland not only as a matter of attitude and effective teaching but also as a matter of identity, Rogelia Pe-Pua, Benedicto Villanueva and Danilo Bv. Tuazon also handled their classes in Filipino. Pe-Pua and Tuazon wrote their M.A. (Psychology) theses in Filipino. Historian Elizabeth Pastores and forester-psychologist Abraham Velasco speak Ilocano. They both wrote their M.A. theses in Filipino (Velasco 1975, Pastores 1981). Their classes were handled in Filipino. Zeus Salazar is an exception. He speaks German and French fluently, apart from his knowledge of Italian and Malay. He has published Filipino translations of Russian works. To the consternation of his English-oriented colleagues, he handles his History and Psychology classes at the university in the national language. Salazar is a native of Bikol and speaks Bikolnon. So does Jose Ma. Bartolome, and so forth and so on. Of course the list includes a minority of Tagalogs, such as Amelia Alfonso and Grace Aguiling-Dalisay, for they are Filipinos also. [For a detailed discussion of the use of the Filipino language in the teaching of psychology from 1965 to 1980 consult Pe (1980)]. Actually, it is pointless to check if Marianita Villariba, Consuelo Paz, Ponciano Bennagen, Augusto Legazpi, Lito Mangulabnan, or Alma Santiago are Tagalogs or not. Colleagues became conscious of the fact that Pe-Pua is non-Tagalog only when she spoke Chinese while trying to locate the University of Hong Kong in connection with the First Asian *sikolohiyang Pilipino* conference held in the Crown Colony. Besides, foreigners and expatriates directly contribute to *sikolohiyang Pilipino* literature. Among the non-Filipino scholars who contributed to the two aforementioned anthologies are Jules de Raedt, Jan J. Loubser, Steven Rood, David Ho, and A. Timothy Church. The concept of an indigenous psychology is precisely rooted in the reality of cultural diversity. Ethnic psychology is a legitimate concern of all social scientists.

Beyond Philippine Shores

The historian Agoncillo (1973) in his book *History of the Filipino People* limits his discussion of Filipino history within the geographic confines of the Philippines, failing to take into account the experience, success and frustration of Filipino communities abroad. Thanks to the Marcos government policy of exporting Filipino manpower, the Filipino can in fact be found all over the world by the '80s: as a domestic helper in Hongkong, as a cultural entertainer in Japan, as an overseas contract worker in the Middle East, as a construction hand or a factory worker in Korea and Taiwan, as a musician in Singapore, and as a nurse or doctor in the United States. The status, nature of employment and working conditions of Filipinos abroad may not exactly be favorable but these do not preclude the observation or conclusion that Filipinos indeed are everywhere.

Further, mainstream historians tend to focus on the coastal cultural communities, virtually setting aside the T'bolis, Bagobos, Tagbanuas and other ethnic groups which continue to struggle for empowerment in the Philippine economic, political and cultural arenas. Granting that a historian who is well aware of ethnic diversity and consciousness can be faulted for such an omission, what are we to expect from others who lack appreciation of indigenous values and culture? Agoncillo has been charged of ignoring the participation of Muslims and Ilocanos in the affairs of the national polity (Azurin 1993). What about the Filipino cultural communities whose voices have not even been heard? It is exactly the problem of voiceless Filipinos, whether an ethnic minority within the Philippines or a powerless worker abroad, which *sikolohiyang Pilipino* seeks to address. Thus a series of networking conferences among indigenous cultural communities towards empowerment, went hand in hand with the establishment of the *Pandaigdigang Katipunan sa Sikolohiyang Pilipino* [International Association for Filipino Psychology] in 1990 with networks in various parts of the world where Filipino communities are found, including Tokyo, Honolulu, Los Angeles and San Francisco, California. *Sikolohiyang Pilipino* seeks to put matters in their proper perspective by explaining Philippine realities and history from the indigenous point of view to come up with a more authentic picture of what and who the Filipino is. After all, even granting that authenticity has to be validated from without, the fact remains that authenticity, in essence, must come from within.

The 1992 Filipino Identity Conference at UC Berkeley and the 1993 conference at Yale University on "Challenges to the Filipino" sponsored by *Sikolohiyang Pilipino sa Amerika* is, no doubt, a welcome development in articulating and affirming Filipino identity. Besides examining Filipino limitations and weaknesses, the conference showed that the movement towards decolonization and indigenization are gaining momentum.

More and more Filipinos are motivated by a quest for community empowerment through decolonization, indigenization and the assertion of Filipino identity. This is particularly evident among Filipino Americans who attend seminars at the Philippine Psychology Research and Training House and visit the different ethnic communities to learn more about Filipino culture and history and in the process, learn and understand themselves better. Filipino Americans are getting more involved in the struggle to reclaim their cultural identity and liberate themselves from the colonial mindframe which have held them captive for so long.

To be sure, *Sikolohiyang Pilipino* is not confined to Philippine shores but has gone across the Pacific. Tagalog is the third most frequently-used language in California and the sixth in the United States. "Pare, me yosi ka ba?" is heard not only in Rio de Janeiro but also from a customs officer in Bahrain.

Training Third World Psychologists

Not any less sensitive but even more intriguing than economic, racial and ethnic concerns are the issues of gender and undue prestige given to foreign-earned degrees. Academic interaction and seminars highlighting developments in psychological research in Philippine colleges and universities, as well as studies on gender and sexism such as Estrada's (1981) investigation of Tagalog as a non-sexist language, were done under the aegis of *sikolohiyang Pilipino*. This is precisely because of dissatisfaction with the established colonial order which favors the Caucasian English-speaking male over the Asian Filipino-speaking female. With the University of Santo Tomas and Manuel L. Quezon University showing the way, more and more Philippine-trained psychologists started *manning* the discipline in different institutions of learning. To use the English transitive verb "to man" in reference to filling the post of psychology department chair is to mislead, if not to be sexist. In the early '80s, as if to dramatize non-dependence on overseas American training and to declare freedom from male dominance in psychology, the psychology departments throughout the country, almost to a *man*, were chaired by Philippine-trained women: Elizabeth Ventura at the University of the Philippines, Evangeline Ortega at the University of

Santo Tomas, Alma de la Cruz at the Ateneo de Manila University, Erlinda Cuizon at Manuel L. Quezon University, Ma. Angeles Lapeña at De La Salle University, Natividad Dayan at Assumption College, Noemi Catalan at Far Eastern University, and Corazon Huvalla at St. Scholastica's College. Not at all unusual in a country which overwhelmingly chose a "plain housewife" for president both in an election and a "People's Power" revolution. It was only in 1985 that the very first non-American-trained psychologist who trained abroad, Ma. Trinidad Crisanto, came back to Manila as the first Filipino to teach psychology in the Philippines after receiving a Ph.D. (Psychology) degree from a French university. Incidentally, Ma. Trinidad Crisanto is also a woman.

Favored with an international outlook, *sikolohiyang Pilipino* is committed to training Filipino scholars in other parts of the globe. The possibilities in overseas training are many. One can study under Minami in Japan, Sinha in India, Sokolov in Russia, Ardilla in Colombia, Diaz-Guerrero in Mexico, or Argyle in England. But studying abroad is a huge investment in time and money, making it more practical to locally train and develop psychologists at the Ph.D. level. Moghaddam and Taylor's (1987) formulae for appropriate training of developing world psychologists take into account the weakness of either of two extremes: isolationism versus advanced training in the West with no consideration for the needs of the developing world. *Sikolohiyang Pilipino* explores various approaches to this concern as the realities of Philippine politics and international fellowships continue to bring Filipinos to New Haven, Los Angeles, Chicago, and Honolulu. There is good news, however. Some attention is now given to Third World issues by a number of leading American universities.

The basic *sikolohiyang Pilipino* training programs are mainly focused on the training of teachers to teach the social sciences in Filipino and with Filipino and Asian orientations. The program for the teaching of psychology in Filipino was evolved and developed from the translation of a psychological work from English to Filipino of an autobiography of a schizophrenic girl in 1971, and the Filipino sourcebook entitled *Diwa: Mga Babasahin sa Sikolohiya* (Enriquez 1971, Enriquez and Antonio 1972) revised and polished through years of actual classroom use until a formal training module was formally developed and tested with a group of psychology teachers and researchers in December 1977 under the direction of Ma. Angeles Guanzon of the University of the Philippines at Clark Air Base. Guanzon subsequently utilized the perspective and training experience at the Foreign Service Institute.

Training workshops on indigenous psychological testing and Filipino values were developed specifically for the industrial sector. Seminars on Philippine-oriented field methods were offered for researchers and community organizers planning to undertake work in the uplands.

4

KAPWA AND THE STRUGGLE FOR JUSTICE, FREEDOM AND DIGNITY

The analysis of human interaction as observed in everyday life and as codified in the language of the people reveals a lot about the people's social psychology and world view. Human interaction is a highly-valued aspect of life in the Philippines. For this reason, social interaction is a meaningful focus of investigation in the process of identifying and analyzing basic concepts of Filipino personality, social psychology, world view and social philosophy.

Levels of Interaction

The Filipino language provides a conceptual distinction in several levels and modes of social interaction. At least eight behaviorally recognizable levels under two general categories in Filipino were identified (Santiago and Enriquez 1976, Santiago 1976):

Ibang-tao or ''Outsider'' Category

Levels: *Pakikitungo* (level of amenities/civility)
           Pakikisalamuha (level of ''mixing'')
           Pakikilahok (level of joining/participating)
           Pakikibagay (level of conforming)
           Pakikisama (level of adjusting)

Hindi ibang-tao or ''One-of-us'' Category

Pakikitungo. In this level, good manners are observed. The social distance is wide but attempts are made to facilitate alliances and still keep social distance

Levels: *Pakikipagpalagayang-loob* (level of mutual trust/rapport)
            Pakikisangkot (level of getting involved)
            Pakikiisa (level of fusion, oneness and full trust)

The distinctions among these eight modes of interaction go beyond the conceptual and theoretical. The eight levels are more than just interrelated modes of interpersonal relations. More importantly, they are levels of interaction which range from the relatively uninvolved civility in *pakikitungo* to the total sense of identification in *pakikiisa*. The different levels of interpersonal relations do not just differ conceptually but behaviorally as well. As an example, Santiago (1976) looked at the language of food, which is really the language of interpersonal relationship in food sharing among the Filipino Bulacan middle class. One is a *bisita* (not one-of-us category) if special dishes are served on guest china. Fernandez (1986) observed that the "dishes served to such a guest are not usually those of the native cuisine (not *paksiw* and *inihaw*) but adapted from that of the colonizers" (*puchero* or *salad*). If one "can share the *sawsawan* (sauce used for dipping/relish) and whatever food there is with the family," and if "one's presence, expected or not, does not occasion a fuss but involves the use of the daily, perhaps plastic, tableware and the customary fare (*pritong galunggong* and *ginisang ampalaya*), then one is *hindi ibang-tao* (one-of-us)."

According to Fernandez (1986), what the Filipino eats, its source and the way it is prepared and served, indicate an intimate, as well as a practical relationship between man and nature. The use of *sawsawan*, for instance, indicates a very relaxed, non-prescriptive relationship between the cook and those cooked for, where the cook does not impose what the flavor of the food should be, allowing the person actually consuming the food to participate in enhancing the flavors by using the *sawsawan*:

> ...food functions to keep this harmony operative. The mutual sharing of functions between the cook and the cooked for and the use of food as a social lubricant, as an infinitely flexible communicator in all kinds of relationships, proves this. Food is better than language, in a way, because it hardly ever offends, and yet its meaning is unmistakable. (Fernandez 1986)

Moreover, food or eating is also a social necessity and a socially-defined phenomenon of sharing which fosters goodwill and friendship. When sharing food, the relationship can either involve the *ibang-tao* (outsider) or *hindi ibang-tao* (one of us) category. It is interesting to note that *kapwa* is the sole concept which embraces both categories.

The domain of interpersonal relations has proved to be theoretically fertile and lexically elaborate in Filipino. All these levels--whether belonging to the *ibang-tao* or *hindi ibang-tao* categories--may be grouped under the heading of *pakikipagkapwa*.

Solidarity in the face of injustice.

Pakikiisa or unity is the highest level of *pakikipagkapwa*.

Thus, anyone looking for a core concept that would help explain Filipino interpersonal behavior cannot help but be struck by the superordinate concept of *kapwa*. It is the only concept which embraces both the categories of "outsider" (*ibang-tao*) and "one of us" (*hindi ibang-tao*).

The Shared Inner Self

Filipino-English dictionaries generally give the words "both" and "fellowbeing" as translations of *kapwa* (Panganiban 1972, Enriquez 1979, de Guzman 1968, Calderon 1957). It should be noted, however, that when asked for the closest English equivalent of *kapwa*, one word that comes to mind is the English word "others." However, the Filipino word *kapwa* is very different from the English word "others." In Filipino, *kapwa* is the unity of the "self" and "others." The English "others" is actually used in opposition to the "self," and implies the recognition of the self as a separate identity. In contrast, *kapwa* is a recognition of shared identity, an inner self shared with others.

Unlike the construct of smooth interpersonal relations (SIR) (Lynch 1961) which is purportedly acquired and preserved principally by *pakikisama*, euphemism and the use of a go-between, the concept of shared inner self (SIS) is rooted in the deeper concept of *kapwa* and *dangal*. Further, while SIR is often referred to as simply a means of avoiding conflict, SIS goes further as it stems from collective values shared with the whole of humanity and the deep respect for the dignity and inherent worth of a fellow human being.

The concept of *kapwa* as a shared inner self turns out to be very important, psychologically as well as philosophically. While *pagtutunguhan* (dealing with/ acting toward) is another term which can be used to refer to all levels of interaction, only the term *pakikipagkapwa* can be used for the same purpose and at the same time indicate an idea, value or conviction which Filipinos consider most important. Besides, *pagtutunguhan* also connotes the most "superficial" level of interaction: the level of amenities, while *pakikipagkapwa* refers to "humanness at its highest level," as Santiago (1976) would put it.

A person starts having *kapwa* not so much because of a recognition of status given him by others but more because of his awareness of shared identity. The *ako* (ego) and the *iba-sa-akin* (others) are one and the same in *kapwa* psychology: *Hindi ako iba sa aking kapwa* (I am no different from others). Once *ako* starts thinking of himself as separate from *kapwa*, the Filipino "self" gets to be individuated in the Western sense and, in effect, denies the status of *kapwa* to the other. By the same token, the status of *kapwa* is also denied to the self.

Brislin (1977) noted that all cultures distinguish between the "in-group" and the "out-group," the "member" and the "non-member," or the "outsider" and the "insider." He surmised that this might be an example of a "universal" or "etic" distinction. Hiroshi Wagatsuma (1982) and Yusihiro Sato (1988) investigated the distinction between *soto* (outside) and *uchi* (inside), the latter of which is also the Japanese word for "family" and "home." Sometimes admired and at other times resented for their intense nationalism, the Japanese *uchi-soto* distinction can be used in understanding the Japanese concept of a *gaijin* or foreigner (usually an American or European). In his work among the homeless in the Sanya district of Tokyo, Grimm (1988) noted a hostile aspect of the *uchi-soto* dichotomy. He claimed that "the *uchi* is, in fact, defined in terms of the *soto* as rival. Without the outside, the inside has no meaning... For Japanese to stand shoulder-to-shoulder with Americans, Europeans, Africans, and other Asians as equals would probably require an invasion from outer space." Grimm must have overstated his case. Humans do not need a face-to-face encounter with extra-terrestrials to sincerely say *ware-ware ningen,* or "we human beings."

Perhaps all cultures have their share of ethnocentrism based on a distinction between the outsider and the insider, and yet there seems to be at least one culture that does not fit this mold perfectly. Ethnocentrism is not *the* concept to study in the Philippines, where even local papers advertise in their classified advertisement sections a preference for foreigners. The social science researcher will go further with a study of xenocentrism, instead.

The idea of inclusion vs. exclusion or membership vs. non-membership is not unknown to the Filipino. He just draws the line in a most flexible manner. For the middle-class Filipino from the Philippine province of Bulacan, the *ibang-tao* (outsider) and the *hindi ibang-tao* (one of us) are both considered *kapwa* (the unity of the one-of-us and the other). In another culture, the concept of membership could be a matter of black and white with no intermediate gray. The Filipino can still accommodate a non-member just as if he were a member. Admittedly not the best form of membership and an "ambiguous category" in the language of the anthropologist Edmund Leach (1964), the *saling-pusa* (informal member) is allowed to break some rules expected to be strictly followed by members. The Filipino would even bend over backwards and let the *saling-pusa* enjoy privileges not particularly enjoyed by the legitimate member. Concepts indigenous to Filipinos are not necessarily peculiar to the Philippines only. However, they have meanings which are close to the Filipino experience. The Filipino concept of *saling-pusa* may be "playful" in tone and may not be found in other cultures, but it is nonetheless significant. It indicates the value attached to the feelings of *kapwa* so that hypocrisy in social interaction is avoided. For example, if a young girl was invited to an important gathering and discovers afterwards that she was only a second choice, she may be hurt, for it would appear that she was a *panakip-butas* (literally "filling a gap").

This is not to say that the Filipino is imprecise about the insider vs. outsider distinction. In fact, the Filipino language has three pronouns for the English "we": a dual "we" (*kita*); an inclusive "we" (*tayo*), and an exclusive "we" (*kami*). *Kita* focuses on the listener in relation to the speaker, *tayo* includes the listener, while *kami* excludes him as referent. The socio-psychological point to remember is a conceptual, behavioral, and value-laden imperative which states that whether *kita, kami,* or *tayo,* the Filipino is dealing with *kapwa* and he thinks and acts accordingly.

Pakikipagkapwa as a conviction emanating from a shared inner self does not simply imply either *pakikitungo* (amenities), *pakikisama* (adjusting), or any of the other modes and levels of interaction.

> *Pakikipagkapwa* is much deeper and profound in its implications. It also means accepting and dealing with the other person as an equal. The company president and the office clerk may not have an equivalent role, status, or income but the Filipino way demands and implements the idea that they treat one another as fellow human beings (*kapwa-tao*). This means a regard for the dignity and being of others.
>
> Aside from the socio-psychological dimension, *pakikipag-kapwa* has a moral and normative aspect as a value and conviction. Situations change and relations vary according to environment. For example, *pakikipagkapwa* is definitely inconsistent with exploitative human transactions. Giving the Filipino a bad deal is a challenge to *kapwa* (*-tao*). (Enriquez 1977)

If only to correct the impression that *pakikipagkapwa* as shared inner self is "other-oriented" just like the lower level of interaction in *pakikisama*, one must be reminded that the Filipino does not always concede. He knows how to resist even when he seems utterly powerless. As demonstrated in the People's Power revolution of 1986, he knows that *pakikibaka* (joining a struggle) is a valid aspect of *pakikipagkapwa* in the face of injustice and adversity.

The complexity of interpersonal relations is recognized in the Tagalog proverb: *"Madali ang maging tao, mahirap ang magpakatao."* (It is easy to be born a *tao* [human], but it is not as easy to be one). The Pampangos deliver essentially the same idea with *"Malagua ing maguing tao, masaquit ing magpacatau."* The Tagalogs concur with *"Kung mahirap ang maging tao, lalong mahirap ang makipagkapwa-tao."* (If it is difficult to be *tao*, it is even more difficult to *makipagkapwa-tao*) (Eugenio 1967).

The Value of *Kagandahang-loob*: Reciprocity or Nobility?

The concept of *kagandahang-loob* (shared inner nobility), once again, displays the characteristic internality/externality dimension of Filipino psychology that confuses so many American-oriented social scientists. The concept is manifested through an act of generosity or *kabutihan*. Thus, one sees *kagandahang-loob* in the act of lending utensils to neighbors or graciously accomodating a guest. But to qualify as *kagandahang-loob*, such acts of generosity must spring spontaneously from the person's goodness of heart or *kabaitan*. A display of *kagandahang-loob* must have no motive save that of kindness and inherent graciousness.

Karangalan: Beyond the Superficiality of *Hiya*

English-oriented social scientists who think Filipinos value *hiya* (commonly translated as "shame" instead of "propriety") must be told about *dangal* or *karangalan*. *Puri, onor,* and *dignidad* are listed as synonyms of *karangalan* (English 1986). The closest English word to *karangalan* is "dignity," but that is only one aspect of the concept. The best way to define the term is to look at the two components of the concept--*dangal* and *puri*. *Puri* or praise/accolade is the external manifestation of *karangalan*. This is given to the person in recognition of a sterling quality or accomplishment. As such it is a recognition that comes entirely from without. The other aspect of *karangalan* is *dangal*. In truth, the word is the root of the concept. On one plane, this refers only to a person's "self-dignity"--the worth of a person as appreciated by the person himself. This self-evaluation may have no relation whatsoever to society's view of him. Hence, a man may go through life in Philippine society puffed up with self-importance, yet his neighbors and peers may see him as just a fool. Sometimes though, this self-evaluation and society's appreciation coincide. In those instances then, a person's *dangal* is recognized through rites of social approval referred to as *parangal*. But again, this aspect of *dangal* owes much to external recognition and thus may even be characterized as another variant of *puri*. That is just one aspect of *dangal*. A more profound placement of *dangal* in Filipino psychology is entirely internal--the intrinsic quality of a person or sector that allows him/them to shine despite the grime of their appearance, environment or status in life. In many instances, this aspect of *dangal* is referred to as "honor" and even "self-respect." It is all these and more. It is the inner strength of a person that allows him to face the rich and the mighty with confidence and resolve.

When a person stakes his *dangal* in defense of or in pursuit of a principle or objective, he is staking no less than his *pagkatao* (personhood); his commitment to that end is therefore total.

Kalayaan: A Matter of Life and Death

Kalayaan is often interpreted as the freedom and license to do as one pleases. This definition carries within itself its own limitation. The concept of freedom as license for a person or group to act in whichever way they please so long as the rights of others are not affected thereby may be adequate, in a sense, especially in the urbanized Philippine setting. For a resident of Metro Manila, for example, his sense

Guarding the sanctity of the ballot.

Karangalan, the Filipino value of honesty and self-dignity.

of *kalayaan* is oftentimes measured within the parameters of existing rules and regulations, of social norms or resources. For the greater portion of the population, however, *kalayaan* means life itself. The freedom to commit a particular act, or the lack of it, determines whether a person or a community survives or perishes. The Aetas of Zambales simply have no choice but to move their *kaingin* fields every so often despite forestry laws to the contrary. The duck raisers of Laguna, in the same manner, must intrude into the fishpens of the bay to gather shells for their flock; otherwise, their livelihood will cease. In this context, then, the Filipino appreciation of *kalayaan* extends beyond the confines of its Western equivalent. The capacity of a person or group to commit an act is determined not by the parameters afforded him by law but by necessity. In many instances then, *kalayaan* carries life and death dimensions.

Katarungan: In Unity and Beyond

Katarungan (social justice) is now invoked as an indispensable condition for peace in Philippine society, in the same breath as food and employment. The movement for ''justice, freedom, and sovereignty,'' which gained the limelight upon the assassination of Benigno Aquino, Jr., underscored the importance of justice as the movement itself was named JAJA, an acronym for ''Justice for Aquino, Justice for All.'' *''Katarungan para kay Lean''* was prominently seen in placards as Filipino nationalists mourned the death of noted student leader Leandro Alejandro. Even the slogan ''national reconciliation'' had to be qualified into ''national reconciliation with justice'' since the fallen dictator must face responsibility for his excesses. The struggle for justice continues as the life of Nemesio Prudente, nationalist president of Polytechnic University of the Philippines, has been twice endangered and human rights lawyers have been murdered. But just as the demand for justice has increased, the debate on the nature of justice has also grown. There are those who look beyond the law and the courts in the search for the constituents of the concept of justice. They equate the realization of the concept to an economic system that would work for the redistribution of the nation's wealth from the hands of the few to the many. And, of course, there are those who would ascribe the same to the domain of the Divine.

Writers on the development of law in Europe and in the Anglo-American tradition speak of law and justice as expressions of culturally rooted values of the people which evolved in the very fabric of social life in the course of their long historical experience. Thus, in those jurisdictions, the concept of what the law is, as a rule, parallels the concept of what is just, the two having come from the same source. The Filipinos, however, are not so fortunate. Law in the Philippine case is a foreign body in an indigenous social life. It was a wholesale grafting of norms conceptualized in foreign communities, as exemplified in Philippine private law which was patterned after the Spanish Civil Code and Philippine public law which was copied from the American Constitutional framework. The Philippine system of laws did not grow from the people. Rather, the people were forced to grow into the law. This resulted in the dissonance between the letter of the law and what the people perceive as right or wrong. Fortunately, the Filipinos seemed to have found a comfortable compromise for an unsettled situation. For as field data from farmers of Bulacan, the urban poor in Diliman, and duck raisers from Laguna show, a balance has been produced between the two systems resulting in a concept of justice which is a combination of the indigenous and the foreign (Enriquez 1987).

As can be expected, the first element of the Filipino concept of *katarungan* is an indictment that the "law is not always just" (Diokno 1985). Moreover, the centrality of law to justice (Avila, Diaz and Rodriguez 1987) is further diminished by the perception that the laudable intents of the statutes may be lost in their implementation; consequently, the oft-repeated lament *"Wala sa batas, nasa pamamalakad ng batas."* *Karapatan, katotohanan* and *katwiran* as elements of *katarungan* flow from the principles laid down by the Anglo-Saxon legal system. They pertain primarily to the conditions necessary for the smooth running of the formal court system. Nevertheless, these three fit well into the Filipino ethos.

It is recognized that people everywhere have certain basic rights, or *karapatan*, that must be respected and defended, the violation of which constitutes injustice. In any case brought to the courts involving alleged violations of *karapatan*, the considerations of fairness and promptness must always be foremost in the minds of the judicial officials. It is also the perception that for justice to be done, the elements of *katotohanan* (truth) and *katwiran* (reason) must always be present in all phases of the court action.

The last two elements, *kapayapaan* and *pagkakaisa* (peace and unity), perceived as making up the concept of justice, derive from the people's *kapwa*-centered value system. These oftentimes dominate the other considerations cited above and are reflected in the Filipino predisposition for seeking compromises to disputes rather than going through the formal court action. The element of justice as peace or *kapayapaan* is often invoked by the phrase *"Diyos na lang ang bahala sa kanya."* The last element is, of course, consensus or *pagkakaisa*. Justice is not what the law says it is but what the people say it should be. These last two elements have colored the Filipino's perception of justice to such an extent that it may be described as "accommodative" rather than "confrontative," a uniquely Filipino way of insuring minimal diturbance to the Filipino core value of *kapwa*.

The Filipino word for law, *batas*, denotes command, order or decree, meanings different from the primary meanings of *katarungan*. The Filipino language seems to indicate that the law is not always just (Diokno 1985). There also seems to be a distinction between the code or the law itself and the implementation of this code. It is in the implementation that justice can be compromised or even negated completely. This distinction is congruent to common perceptions that the current system of implementing laws does not provide justice for all; instead it provides justice only for the rich and powerful. Precisely because of this observation, one finds it reasonable to argue that those who have "less in life should have more in law."

Another dimension of *katarungan* is the recognition of certain basic rights, or *karapatan*. There is a strong belief that there exist certain basic rights, in particular the right to oneself and to one's own (e.g., physical being, possessions, pesonal affairs) and the right to one's means of livelihood with which others should not interfere (Silliman 1982). This view is confirmed by Machado's (1979) and Silliman's (1982) finding that most disputes are personal rather than public in nature.

The significance of this dimension of *katarungan* can be seen in the root of the word *karapatan* which is *dapat*, meaning appropriate and correct. These meanings are also the root of the term *katarungan*, indicating the close relation of the two concepts in the Filipino value-system.

The emphasis on personal rights indicates a personal notion of justice. That is, conflicts or situations of injustice are perceived as being against oneself; justice is obtained when personal redress has been made to oneself or when one's personal circumstances have been restored to their previous condition (Silliman 1982, Machado 1979). A personal notion of justice, however, also applies to social situations in which classes of individuals are involved in the distribution of benefits or burdens and not only to individual cases (Silliman 1983).

TABLE III

Kagandahang-Loob: Pakikipagkapwa as Pagkamakatao [Nobility, Benevolence & Compassion in Kapwa Psychology]		
CORE VALUE	**KAPWA** (shared identity) {Pagkatao}		
Linking Socio-Personal Value	**Kagandahang-loob** (shared humanity) {Pagkamakatao}		
Associated Social Values	**karangalan** (dignity)	**katarungan** (justice)	**kalayaan** (freedom)
Reductionist Interpretation	"social acceptance"	"social equity"	"social mobility"

Beyond *Pakikisama*: Equity and Fairness

A fundamental component of the concept of *katarungan* is fairness, which means giving equal treatment to everyone, rich or poor, powerful or weak. Fairness is derived from the idea that *katarungan* includes the idea of "appropriateness." Where power and privilege are concentrated in the hands of a few, achieving justice implies the operation of fairness and "appropriateness." (Diokno 1982, Silliman 1982).

In the settlement of disputes, access to justice should be quick and inexpensive. However, only the rich can afford lengthy and costly proceedings. The prevailing judicial system is partial to them.

The will of the majority is integral to the concept of fairness. Since the poor comprise the majority, their interest should be represented. Although rich and poor should be treated equally, their interests are clearly perceived as different. In case of conflict, the side of the poor should be given more weight because they are the majority. If a system is to be fair, and therefore *makatarungan* (just), the majority should be heeded instead of the powerful minority.

Katotohanan and *Katwiran*: Truth and Reason

Two concepts related to the value of *katarungan* are *katotohanan* (truth) and *katwiran* (reason). In the implementation of justice, *katotohanan* shields one from false accusations. Take, for instance, a case where a person is accused of a certain crime. A just decision on his case would require that the truth be ascertained. Furthermore, for a situation to be just, there should be absolutely no deception, falsity, cover-up, whitewashing, or the like. For *katarungan* to be realized, there should be untarnished *katapatan* or honesty. *Katotohanan* is at the core of *katapatan*.

As it is used in different Philippine languages, the primary meaning of *katarungan* is reason, indicating the close relationship between *katwiran* and *katarungan*. Silliman (1983) explains: "Used in the context of explaining why someone takes a complaint to a village official, *katarungan* implies 'right' (just) reason or just cause with the implication that the others should readily see the 'justness' of one's case."

Pagkakaisa: Justice in Unity or Consensus

The Filipino concept of *katarungan* operates at the highest level of social interaction, *pagkakaisa* (unity/being one with others). *Pagkakaisa* implies a consensus or an agreement among all parties involved in a situation. In the case of a dispute, for instance, the formal intervention by the hands of the law to settle what is perceived to be an injustice is not needed. Steps are taken by the parties involved, like having a

Kawalang-galang (disrespect) towards the environment: Illegal logging destroys the environment and the material and economic bases of the culture of those depending on it.

Justice for all: Not only for the rich and powerful.

dialogue to clarify issues, to reach a compromise to which all agree. This consensus is sufficient, or at the very least necessary, to say that justice has been done. This is similar to what is referred to as an "amicable settlement of disputes." Dissent or opposition, especially by the majority, would indicate that their sentiments are not being considered. Therefore there can be no agreement and there can be no justice.

Pagkakaisa is also the highest level of interpersonal interaction possible. It can be said that being one with another is a full realization of *pakikipagkapwa*. At this level of interaction, there is total trust and identification among the parties involved. The "shared inner self" in *kapwa* psychology has a reflexive quality, such that what is good for one is shared and is good for the other, what would be to the detriment of one is accepted in fact as detrimental to the other. Being one with another, a person will not act or decide in any way that would injure the dignity of another person, precisely because he has complete appreciation of the other person's being as if it were an extension of one's own self.

In spirit, therefore, with *pagkakaisa*, no one can be better off than the other in any way. This is a precondition of *katarungan*, which seems to be over and beyond the ordinary concept of fairness. *Pagkakaisa*, and also *katarungan*, however, are viewed as normative conditions. The context of Filipino society is perceived as inequitable; the wealthy and the powerful are clearly better off, even with regard to access to justice. The current judicial system is popularly perceived as providing justice only for the rich and powerful.

Settlements, therefore, are not necessarily accepted as fair or just. The so-called agreements are often determined by the comparative power of the disputants rather than by the demands of justice. The rich and powerful will always have the edge. They will always have better bargaining positions than ordinary folk. A just or fair outcome can be expected in settlements only when the disputants are nearly equal in social status, i.e., in money, power, and influence. *Pagkakaisa* then remains an ideal objective. The lower levels of interaction, *pakikisama* and *pakikibagay*, become the compromise norm.

Kapayapaan (Peace): Consequence of *Katarungan* as Unity

The Filipino concept of *katarungan* is accommodative, as indicated by two significant characteristics of this concept. First is the value given to *kapayapaan* along with *katarungan*, giving the latter a non-confrontative quality. This is most clearly reflected in situations when one is a victim of injustice by another. The injustice is sometimes resolved with a *"Diyos na lang ang bahala sa kanila."* The acceptance, as part of social reality, of the unwanted system of *"palakasan,"* is a manifestation of this non-confrontative, and therefore accommodative nature of the concept of *katarungan*.

Filipino Psychology: From the Filipino, For the Filipino

Kapayapaan (peace) as a consequence of justice

The pervasiveness of resorting to settlements or mediation of disputes despite the existence of a formal litigation system also underscores the significance ascribed to *kapayapaan*. Settlements, aside from being quicker and cheaper than court litigations, increase the likelihood of reestablishing amicable and cordial relationships between disputants.

It should be noted, however, that settlements are not always accepted as just, and that *kapayapaan* is never equated with *katarungan*. Settlement becomes an acceptance or a yielding to a greater power, to *palakasan*, which is understood as unjust. *Kapayapaan* then is maintained at the surface level. *Ibang-tao* (not one-of-us) interaction is held at the level of *pakikisama*.

The second characteristic is that *katarungan* is graded, that is, there are different levels or gradations of justice. This characteristic seems to have evolved from the preceding quality of non-confrontativeness. The recognition and acceptance of prevailing unjust systems allow for a compromise with justice, giving in to the powers-that-be to some degree to be able to attain some acceptable degree of justice. The people are, in fact, *nakikibagay* with the unjust implementation of the legal system.

The often-heard plea for *"maski kaunting katarungan lamang"* (a little justice) is reflective of this graded justice. Thus, it is never the case that a situation is either *"makatarungan"* or *"di-makatarungan."* These two exist as extremes, the former being the ideal, the latter the status quo. Between these two are levels with which one has to be satisfied as a compromise, having in mind some other value--*kapayapaan*.

Care, however, must be taken not to generalize that this element is equally perceived by the different subcultures in Philippine society. This apprehension is borne out by the fact that the respondents promoting such a concept belong to lowland communities which are relatively free from the tension and strife evident in the other areas in the countryside. Further investigation of this element in areas where militancy among the populace is exhibited is necessary to determine conclusively if the perception of *kapayapaan* as an element of justice is present across ethnic groups.

Relations of domination and exploitation are ultimately responsible for the perpetuation of injustice in Philippine society, particularly among the poor and underprivileged. Justice, like education, health care, and law, is essentially a political and economic phenomenon that cannot be divorced from its societal context.

5

THE FILIPINIZATION
OF PERSONALITY THEORY

Sikolohiyang Pilipino's strong commitment to the development of national identity and consciousness inspired a renewed critical interest in the scientific study of the Filipino personality. In fact, one important meaning of *sikolohiyang Pilipino* is *sikolohiya ng mga Pilipino* or Filipino psychology and character. However, studies on national character have long been suspect because of methodological problems and the risk of stereotyping a people.

The concepts of national character in general and Filipino personality in particular are wrought with difficulties. Bartolome (1985) maintained that the very "idea of a Filipino personality...can work against or even be used against the Filipinos themselves." He was critical of the way the Marcos regime was apparently endorsing legitimate pride in Filipino national heritage and culture "by resurrecting *barangays* and other ancient concepts on the pretext that they are great or worthy examples of a great past" but actually exploiting nationalist sentiments with the aim of "obscuring the more compelling social realities" of the nation.

The Philippines after Marcos remained unmindful of Bartolome's warning. In fact, "understanding the Filipino personality and character" took a sinister turn once more, this time in the familiar form of blaming the victim for his sorry state by starting with the assumption that the worst enemy of the Filipino is himself.

A distinction should be made between the concepts of "personality" and *pagkatao* (Enriquez 1979). Concern with the Filipino character as if the Filipino were an object of analysis from the outside by an outsider, or alternatively by an objective insider, jibes very well with the concept of personality which is rooted in the concept of "persona"--a mask which can be observed from the outside. However, *pagkatao* is perhaps best rendered as "personhood." *Pagkataong Pilipino*, therefore, asserts the shared humanity and the *kapwa* psychology of the Filipino.

Billed by media as an attempt to know "what's wrong and what's right with the Filipino," the Philippine Senate on September 18, 1987 approved Resolution No. 10 sponsored by Senators Leticia Ramos-Shahani, Alberto Romulo, and Ernesto Maceda. The resolution directed "the committee on education, arts and culture, and the committee on social justice, welfare and development to conduct a joint inquiry into the strengths and weaknesses of the character of the Filipino with a view to solving the social ills and strengthening the nation's moral fiber." The result was a 68-page report in English by a task group headed by Patricia B. Licuanan of the Ateneo de Manila University submitted to Senator Shahani on April 27, 1988. In spite of all the good intentions and the stated aim of coming up with a balanced picture, the resulting image reflected more of the colonial instead of the indigenous identity of the Filipino. This is understandable because they relied on a review of the English language literature on the Filipino character, as well as a token focused-group discussion in "a depressed urban poor resettlement area in Dasmariñas, Bagong Bayan, Cavite."

Indigenous Identity and the Colonial Image of the Filipino

A scientific and balanced look at personality and culture studies in the Philippines was an important concern for *sikolohiyang Pilipino* precisely because of the need to correct the imbalance in a situation where the Filipino is primarily characterized from the judgmental and impressionistic point of view of the colonizers. In addition, the native Filipino invariably suffers from the comparison in not too subtle attempts to put forward Western behavior patterns as models for the Filipino. As Lawless (1969) puts it, "in the case of Lynch's comparison, is it not better to be frankly honest than socially ingratiating? And in Nurge's comparison, is it not better to have a 'true' verbal description of reality than a deceptive one?" Even Bulatao's metaphor of a "split-level" bungalow relegates the Filipino to the basement and assigns the American to the upper level. Be that as it may, the continuing interest in identity and national consciousness is not a monopoly of psychologists of the *sikolohiyang Pilipino* persuasion. What makes *sikolohiyang Pilipino* different is its intense pursuit of developing the indigenous national culture and its program of using the indigenous language in its conferences, research, teaching, and publication.

The massive influence of the United States of America on education, religion, commerce, politics, and the mass media predisposes the Filipino to adopt the colonial viewpoint in studying and explaining the Filipino psyche. Normally, the importation of an alien perspective provides a measure of objectivity to a research since the scholar is not enmeshed and bound by the culture he is studying. The Philippine experience, however, was different. Most of the American-trained social scientists did not only appraise the data that came in but also stood in judgment of their worth and importance, using American categories and standards. The supposedly Filipino values or concepts were lifted, as it were, from the cultural milieu and examined according to inappropriate alien categories, resulting in a distorted and erroneous appraisal of indigenous psychology.

Sikolohiyang Pilipino is not simply concerned with the image of the Filipino or the motive behind invidious comparisons. The evaluation of Filipino values and patterns of behavior was a question of national interest:

> Comparisons are usually resorted to in explaining the Filipino way of life to strangers. The basis for comparison, the interpretative scheme, should be critically evaluated especially if the observations are made by the strangers themselves. The issue here is not simply the nationality of the stranger observer or his length of exposure to the Filipino way of life. The question, rather, is: from whose national interest should Philippine culture be evaluated? (Samson 1980)

The colonial character of Philippine social science, developed and written in the English language, is particularly and painfully evident in studies of Filipino "national character" and values. The majority of these studies rely uncritically on a borrowed language, inapplicable categories of analysis, and a token use of the local language and culture. Designations for supposedly indigenous values and patterns of behavior include terms and expressions from English (e.g., "Filipino time"), Spanish (e.g., *delicadeza, amor propio*), and a curious mixture of English and Spanish (e.g., *mañana habit*). If ever Philippine terms are used at all, they simply function as mere labels, more often than not, with very little research and understanding of their deeper significance and content. Moreover, indigenous terms most often found in American-oriented English language researches were drawn primarily from the Tagalog language of Central Luzon (e.g., *bahala na, ningas kugon,* etc.). A smattering of concepts was occasionally plucked from different regions of the country (e.g., *mahay* and *gaba* from Cebuano) but as a whole, the analysis and interpretation of Filipino values is substantially keyed to a foreign language and perspective.

The risks involved in this widespread practice are many. These studies usually conclude by identifying supposed Philippine values and patterns of behavior. More often than not, however, the studies fail to see the values in terms of the Filipino world view, experience, and milieu. The organization and logic of the value as it is viewed from the indigenous perspective is ignored.

The distorted view of Filipino values becomes even worse when the English-oriented researcher, in affixing a label to a supposed value, simply scans the list of indigenous terms which presumably refer to the same and plucks out the one which seems to describe that value best. Without prior study and respect for the language involved, the researcher may be dealing with a list that is both inappropriate and inadequate. The resulting labelling, therefore, may be incorrect, as is often the case.

Language has its own logic; hence, we cannot afford to ignore such a rich resource. The use of the language of the masses in the writing and dissemination of scientific reports makes socio-political sense. However, it is more important to recognize that in the language lie many pieces of the Filipino culture puzzle. The continued denial of the proper role of the indigenous language in social science research and its diminution as a mere source of convenient labels and as a facade for Filipinization and respectability only results at best in an unstructured collection of indigenous terms affixed to supposedly Filipino values. Thus, a listing of Filipino values is now conveniently available for scholars and tourists alike who somehow feel that they have a better understanding of the Filipino personality on the basis of their readings of such exotica as *amor propio, bahala na* and *pakikisama*:

> The token use of Filipino concepts and the local language has led to the identification of some supposedly Filipino national values. Among the frequently-mentioned values are *hiya* (shame), *pakikisama* (yielding to the leader or majority), *utang na loob* (gratitude), *amor propio* (sensitivity to personal affront) and *bayanihan* (togetherness in common effort). Some regional values which have been recognized include *maratabat* (a complex combination of pride, honor and shame), *balatu* (sharing of one's fortune), *ilus* (sharing surplus food), *kakugi* (meticulousness and attention to detail), *patugsiling* (compassion), *kalulu* (empathy), *hatag gusto* (generosity), *paghiliupod* (faithfulness in need or plenty), and *pagsinabtanay* (fidelity with one's promises). (Elequin 1974)

Apparently, then, the emphasis in this kind of research is the search for the English equivalent of the indigenous term. The label is fitted, squeezed, and pushed into the mind-set concomitant to the foreign equivalent. The term's real significance in the Philippine context is diminished, if not entirely lost. More sinister still, by lifting the indigenous term from its milieu and slapping it on a supposed value, the researcher can attach whatever significance he may assign to the latter. In the hands of a Western-oriented researcher whose motivation in doing the research may concededly be academic, such privilege may, unwittingly, still be supportive of oppressive ends. The inappropriateness of this dangerous approach to the study of Filipino values can best be seen in the concepts most often treated and highlighted in researches of this ilk: *hiya, utang na loob*, and *pakikisama*. Many social scientists have studied them as separate values and in isolation from all others. Moreover, popular writers, taking their cue from these studies, often situate these values at the very seat of the Filipino's personality, the absence of which they deem fatal to the former's ethnicity.

The functionalist value studies popularized by the Institute of Philippine Culture and referred to by Robert Lawless (1969) as the "Ateneo approach" was controversial, to say the least. Dissatisfied with "personalized accounts of behavior with only anecdotal supporting materials," Lawless warned against the "replication of uniformity" and the selection of "whatever data fit expectations," making it difficult to correct "early misimpressions."

Even granting "authenticity" to "common Asian and feudal-agricultural values," Andrew B. Gonzalez (1982) saw what "seemed to be labeling activities" in the earlier attempts by Lynch and Hollnsteiner. Bennagen (1985) was forthright in his criticism of what he called "verbal Filipinization, that is, the search for Filipino words while using an essentially structural-functionalist perspective." In a call for the full use of Filipino in the social sciences, *verbal Filipinization* was characterized as *malapustisong gamit ng wika* or "token use of the Filipino language" (Enriquez 1981). The token use of indigenous vocabulary should not be confused with the forming of appropriate theory.

The functionalist approach is not without defenders. Convinced that the surface values of *hiya, pakikisama,* and *utang na loob* "certainly play a strong *functional* role in Filipino daily life, notwithstanding the fact that *kapwa* plays a 'superior' *conceptual* role," Tennant (1987) insisted that "as halting and faltering as the process may be, people still communicate face to face, not core to core." However, he did not deny that communication and social interaction should be interpreted on the basis of core meanings.

In Search of Core Meanings: The Role of Language

If one must communicate, language definitely helps. Using the Filipino language, ones sees *hiya, utang na loob* and *pakikisama* merely as surface values, readily apparent attributes appreciated and exhibited by many Filipinos. In addition, these three are recognized as a triad whose legs emanate from a single trunk, the actual core value of the Filipino personality. This core value has been identified as *kapwa*. Surface values therefore are not free-standing values which anyone can assume at will. The core value must be cultivated and understood first before the full meaning of the surface values can become apparent and appreciated.

Moreover, the use of the indigenous language led to the identification of an underlying precondition for the existence of the surface values, that is to say, the concept and value of *pakiramdam*. The function of this value is to act as the processor, or pivot, which spins off the surface values from the core value of *kapwa*. A person without *pakiramdam* cannot possibly have *pakikisama* and *utang na loob*. Similarly, one cannot expect *hiya* from someone who has no *pakiramdam*.

Perhaps this value system can be best illustrated in the popular Filipino conception of the *masamang tao* (bad or evil person). The *masamang tao* can be characterized as one who does not exhibit the accommodative values of *hiya, utang na loob*, and *pakikisama*. The denial or absence of each of these accommodative values is labelled: 1) the *walang pakisama* (one inept at the level of adjustment); 2) the *walang hiya* (one who lacks a sense of *karangalan* or honor/propriety); and 3) the *walang utang na loob* (one who lacks adeptness in respecting a shared dignity, *karangalan* and *kagandahang-loob*).

The person characterized as *walang pakiramdam* is of course worse off than any of the three "evil" characters mentioned above. It is definitely unfortunate, to put it mildly, to be afflicted with such an inadequacy. This particularly sad state is captured in one Filipino word: *manhid* (numb/absence of feeling).

However, such a character pales in comparison beside one who is *walang kapwa*:

> One argument for the greater importance of *kapwa* in Filipino thought and behavior is the shock or disbelief that the Filipino registers when confronted with one who is supposedly *walang kapwa(-tao)*. If one is *walang pakisama*, others might still say, "He would eventually learn" or "Let him be; that's his prerogative." If one is *walang hiya*, others say, "His parents should teach him a thing or two." If one is *walang utang na loob* others might advise, "Avoid him." But if one is *walang kapwa tao*, people say "He must have reached rock bottom. *Napakasama na niya*. He is the worst." (Enriquez 1978)

The surface values can vary cross-culturally. Even the relative importance attached to the pivotal value of *pakikiramdam* is determined by cultural imperatives. Not so with *kapwa*. In the Philippine value system, *kapwa* is at the very foundation of human values. This core value then determines not only the person's personality but more so his personhood or *pagkatao*. Without *kapwa*, one ceases to be a Filipino. One also ceases to be human.

Pakikiramdam: The Pivotal Aspect of *Kapwa*

Pakikiramdam is the pivotal value of shared inner perception. It refers to heightened awareness and sensitivity. Mataragnon (1987) characterized *pakikiramdam* as "feeling for another," a kind of emotional *a priori*. *Pakikiramdam* is an active process involving great care and deliberation manifested in "hesitation to react, inattention to subtle cues, and non-verbal behavior in mental role-playing (if I were in the other's situation, how would I feel)" (Mataragnon 1987).

Using *pakikiramdam*, a person seeks to clarify an ambiguous and therefore critical situation to arrive at an appropriate response. It is a legitimate move leading to *pakikiisa* (being one with others); later, to being able to identify with another's being; and ultimately, to being able to share complete trust.

Pakikiramdam is necessarily tied to the operation of all Filipino surface values. Regarding *pakikisama*, Mataragnon (1987) writes, "A person who knows how to get along well with others is one who is *'magaling makiramdam'* (good in sensing cues)." She sees circumspection in *pakiramdam*:

> ...*hiya* demand[s] that one conducts oneself in a circum-spect manner, e.g., with *pakikiramdam. Kahihiyan* could be avoided by sizing up the situation first and watching how others react. In being considerate and behaving as *kapwa*, one tries not to cause *kahihiyan* to others; in saving face and preserving *amor propio*, one tries not to bring *kahihiyan* upon oneself. In all this, *pakikiramdam* may be seen as some kind of golden rule.

Without *pakiramdam*, there is no sense of time and *kalooban*. Thus, *utang na loob* is not only reduced to reciprocity but also vanishes completely:

> It is with one's *loob* (being) that one feels. One could have a debt and pay it back in business-like fashion without *utang na loob*. On the other hand, the emotional component is at a maximum in *utang na loob* reciprocity...Voluntary initiation of the action is also extremely important, for the spirit in which a service is rendered, the giving of self that is involved, lends an emotional content to the relationship that is lacking in contractual and quasi-contractual reciprocity (Lynch 1973). Without *pakikiramdam*, one cannot acquire a sense of *utang na loob*; neither can one know when and how to express this sense of gratitude.

The improvisatory character of *pakikiramdam* is operative in *bahala na*:

> *Bahala na* strikes a curious relationship with *pakikiramdam*. At first sight, it appears that *bahala na* is reckless and fatalistic while *pakikiramdam* is careful and humanistic...Lagmay men-tions the "improvisatory personality" of the Filipino which allows him to be comfortable with unstructured, indefinite, and unpredict-able situations. It is this same "improvisatory personality" that is at work in *pakikiramdam*. (Mataragnon 1987)

The Centrality of *Pakiramdam* in Behavioral and Interpersonal Domains

The recognition of a parallelism between the triad of accommodative surface values and the behavioral-phenomenological domain of *biro-lambing-tampo-* (tease/joke-sweetness/caress-resent/disappoint) generates a number of fascinating hypotheses. *Biro* (joke/tease) is most relevant to the domain of the surface value of *hiya*. The initial tension attributable to *hiya* during interpersonal encounters, which is most likely to occur at levels of interactions below *pakikipagpalagayang-loob* can be neutralized by a *biro*. Even the expression *"Napahiya ka ano?"* can actually be a *biro* disguised as chastisement. *Biro* and *hiya* are actually correlated though not ordinarily recognized as such. In a culture which uses teasing as a form of socialization or even as a strategy for establishing rapport, this relationship is easier to apprehend.

Even less intimately related and often thought of as unrelated are the surface value of *pakikisama* and the behavioral pattern of *lambing* (sweetness/underlying fondness). *Lambing* behavior is more likely to be observed in situations where *pakikisama* is operative. There are situational constraints to the manifestations of *lambing*. For example, it is supposed to be absent in *pakikisama* among male *barkada* (indigenous peer group). However, it can be argued that *lambing* is simply manifested in different ways depending upon sex, status, age, nature of relationship, and the like. Similarly, *tampo* is the behavioral pattern and phenomenological feeling most frequently associated with perceived disregard for *utang na loob*. Again, the two are not normally thought of as related, and yet *tampo* is the first thing felt and/or manifested in the face of a supposedly unrecognized or unreciprocated *utang na loob*. Basic to all these is the value of *pakiramdam*. Table 4 summarizes the relationship among the values.

TABLE IV

Pakiramdam: Pakikipagkapwa as Pagkatao [Shared Inner Perception, Self and Identity in **Kapwa** Psychology]		
CORE VALUE	**KAPWA** (shared identity)	{*Pagkatao*}
Pivotal Inter - personal Value	*Pakiramdam* {*Pakikipagkapwa-tao*} (shared inner perception)	
Colonial/ Accommodative Surface Value	*hiya* (propriety/ dignity) — *utang na loob* (gratitude/ solidarity)	*pakikisama* (companionship/ esteem)
Associated Behavior Pattern	*biro* (joke) — *lambing* (sweetness)	*tampo* (affective disappointment)
Confrontative Surface Value	*bahala na* (determination)	*sama/lakas ng loob* (resentment/guts)	*pakikibaka* (resistance)

The Internality-Externality Dimension in *Pakikiramdam*

Dissecting the term *pakikiramdam* yields two related concepts. The first would be *paki-* which is an affixation indicating a request or a plea. The second would be *ramdam*, a variation of *damdam* which means to feel. Although *damdam* and *dama* would both mean "to feel," this English equivalent does not consider the externality-internality dimensions of feeling. Strictly speaking, *dama* is external in quality; that is, having a social dimension, concerning one's interactions with other people.

Pakidama would therefore be external in character. On the other hand, *damdam* is internal in nature; that is, it involves one's *"loob,"* a recognition of a person's individuality.

PORTRAIT OF THE COMPLIANT FILIPINO

Readily-observable surface values are often mistaken for distinguishing attributes of the Filipinos as opposed to other nationalities. That may cause a bit of confusion as was mentioned earlier, as these values may vary among the different ethnic groupings of the archipelago. Moreover, the misconception that the triad of *hiya*, *utang na loob*, and *pakikisama* constitutes the entirety of surface values is fostered by colonial social science. One researcher even went as far as identifying a surface value as a Filipino "goal, purpose, and objective." While bordering on the absurd, the idea is perpetuated in English social science textbooks (e.g., Hunt, Quisumbing, Espiritu, Costelo & Lacar 1987). The *hiya-utang na loob-pakikisama* triad forms only one category, the accommodative surface values. Its counterpart grouping may be referred to as the confrontative surface values.

As can be gathered from the adjective, accommodative values function primarily to maintain the status quo either on an individual or group basis. Over the years, American-oriented researchers have seized on this category to such an extent that all other values have been pushed to the sidelines. Because of the sheer visibility of studies made on the subject, translation labels for each of them have seeped into popular usage and have been taken as appropriate.

Hiya got bandied about as "shame" or "embarassment." *Utang na loob* got to be known as "reciprocity." But no one really got carried away except when *pakikisama* was elevated to the status of a value and passed off as a Filipino "goal, purpose, and objective."

Unlike the seeming institutionalization of accommodative values, the confrontative values were either ignored or misinterpreted outright. The popularization of *bahala na* as fatalism is a case in point since the basic confrontative meaning of the concept was not duly recognized. Another confrontative value, *lakas ng loob*, never came to the fore as did *utang na loob*, another *loob*-related value found in the other category.

This oversight seems linked to the observation that *utang na loob* happens to be consistent with subservience and servility. The same is the case with *pakikibaka*, the last of the triad of confrontative values. This concept was paid only scant attention, perhaps by being "out of place" in a society widely presented as "servile," "fun loving" and "hospitable." Increasingly, however, this triad of confrontative values is now beginning to get the attention and appreciation due them.

The Moral Dimension of *Hiya*

One of the earlier studies done on *hiya* (propriety/dignity) was by Sibley (1965), an anthropologist with the Philippine Studies Program at the University of Chicago. He went to the Philippine island of Panay and studied *huya* (which is equivalent to *hiya* among the Tagalogs, according to his study). Sibley came to the conclusion that *hiya* is "social" in character. He failed to appreciate the moral dimension of the concept precisely because he did not pay attention to a major characteristic of the indigenous language: the system of affixation.

The system of affixation is a very important aspect of the Filipino language which should not be glossed over by root-word-oriented analysts of Philippine values. This distinction can be illustrated by citing an attempt by Sibley to bolster his claim with a Tagalog *salawikain* (saying) which was reportedly used to refer to a woman who committed suicide to escape *hiya: Nahiya sa tao; sa Diyos ay hindi.*

His translation was erroneous. One should not confuse *nahiya* with *nakakahiya*. When one says *"Nakakahiya sa tao; sa Diyos ay hindi,"* one is concerned with the social, instead of the moral, aspect of the behavior. A loose but idiomatic translation of this would be "It's a shameful sin against society but not against God." Obviously, this cannot be said of suicide. However, the saying *"Nahiya sa tao, sa Diyos ay hindi"* is ironic; it precisely means *"Dapat ay mahiya din sa Diyos,"* or "she should not have sinned against God either." This is clearly a moral injunction missed by Sibley. The affix *na-* says something very different from what *nakaka-* implies. *"Nahiya sa tao; sa Diyos ay hindi"* implies *"Dapat ay mahiya sa Diyos,"* thereby attaching a socio-moral significance to the concept of *hiya.* Sibley missed the point altogether by ascribing to the word *nahiya* the meaning appropriate to *nakakahiya.*

In fact, the slang *"dyahe"* came up in the '70s to communicate the purely social aspect of the concept of *"hiya."* *"Dyahe"* is actually an inversion of the syllables of *hi-ya* to *ya-hi,* coupled with a change in the initial sound from "h" to "dy." Wearing bell bottom trousers when everyone else is sporting a semi*baston* (slightly tight-fitting pants) is *dyahe.* The sanction is social. The moral question is not involved at all. Sibley got the meaning of *dyahe* but missed out on *hiya* altogether. To think that it was just a matter of distinguishing the affix *na-* from *nakaka-.* What more if he were to encounter the nominal form of *hiya* in *kahihiyan?*

Armando Bonifacio (1976) was right when he called attention to the fact that *napahiya* is not *nakakahiya* and certainly not *"ikinahihiya."* Aside from *na-* and *nakaka-*, we have *napa-* and *ikina-*, not to mention *ka-an*. Salazar's (1981) ground-breaking study of affixation and *hiya* supported once more the importance of the externality-internality dimension in the analysis of Filipino psychology. He identified the two aspects of *hiya*, namely, the *labas* (external/interpersonal) and the *loob* (internal/being). The *labas* aspect of *hiya* is the natural domain of behavioral psychology, as in *hiyain*, *ikahiya*, and *manghiya*. Earlier studies on *hiya* captured the external aspect of the concept and characteristically ignored the more important internal or *loob* aspect.

On the other hand, the *loob* aspect of *hiya* is related to qualities and the foundation or terminal value of *karangalan* as in *mahiyain*, *kahiya-hiya*, and *hiyang-hiya*. The *labas*-related meanings also have a social dimension, pertaining to social interaction such as *pakikitungo*, *pakikisalamuha*, *pakikibagay*, and *pakikisama*. The *loob* related meanings, on the other hand, have an emotional dimension pertaining to the intensity of one's feeling of *hiya*. Furthermore, the *labas*-oriented affix, aside from its social dimension, also denotes that *hiya* can be a voluntary, conscious act (*sinasadya*), or involuntary, beyond one's volition (*di-sinasadya*).

The Filipino Self-Image and the "Blessings" of *Utang na Loob*

Another surface value given inordinate attention in the Western-oriented studies of Philippine values is *utang na loob* (gratitude/solidarity). Charles Kaut (1961) admitted that *utang na loob* is not uniquely Filipino; it can also be found in Washington, D.C., except that Americans value *kaliwaan* (direct exchange) more. Concepts such as *lakas ng loob*, *kusang loob*, and *sama ng loob* were summarily ignored because of the minimal appreciation given to the Filipino language and the lack of appreciation of the meaning and significance of the theoretically fertile concept of *loob*. One can state in detail all the reasons why "American aid" is a form of imperialism (Hayter 1971); if *utang na loob* is a paramount value to an extent where *lakas ng loob*, *kusang loob*, *sama ng loob*, and other *loob*-related concepts are ignored, then the Filipino should be grateful indeed.

The problems with the token use of Filipino psychological concepts in the context of a Western analysis that relies on the English language and English categories of analysis are many. It no doubt can lead to the distortion of Philippine social reality and the furtherance of the mis-education of the Filipinos. It is no coincidence that Kaut (1961) hit upon *utang na loob* (debt of "gratitude") as a key concept for the analysis of Tagalog interpersonal relations, considering that *utang na*

> *loob* is just one among many psycho-social concepts that relate
> to the theoretically fertile concept of *loob*. We have *sama ng*
> *loob* (''resentment''), *kusang loob* (''initiative''), *lakas ng*
> *loob* (''guts''), and many others. Samonte (1973) needed no
> less than three pages just to list down such concepts. In
> addition, Kaut admitted that ''debt of gratitude'' is not
> altogether unknown in Washington, D.C. Even Americans
> recognize *utang na loob*, they just happen to prefer *kaliwaan*
> or immediate pay-offs whenever possible. To argue that *utang*
> *na loob* is a Filipino value is therefore misleading to say the
> least, and dangerous at best. *Utang na loob* would be
> convenient in perpetuating the colonial status of the Filipino
> mind. (Enriquez 1977)

Perhaps it is not a coincidence that out of a long list of *loob*-related concepts, *utang na loob* was singled out and perpetuated as an important aspect of the Filipino national self-image. In addition, the English-language interpretations of *utang na loob* as reciprocity happen to be useful in promoting the image of the colonizer as benefactor.

Kaut's 1961 study was misused and overdrawn without due regard to the dangers of reductionism when the interpretation of *utang na loob*, in terms of direct exchange of goods and favors, became *the* interpretation of *utang na loob*. Since *utang na loob* is definitely not so gross and scheming as the pragmatic ''you scratch my back and I'll scratch yours,'' it is inaccurate and misleading to focus on the gift, the acceptance, the repayment, and the elements of need and surplus.

Although Kaut also had occasion to translate *utang na loob* into ''debt of gratitude,'' still the mercantilist interpretation of the concept persisted until it got tagged as ''reciprocity.'' Hollnsteiner, another social scientist, pushed the erroneous interpretation even further by claiming that the interaction emanating from *utang na loob* is ''contractual.'' While recognizing the significant role of ''emotions'' (her closest gloss to *loob*), she claims that the recipient is compelled ''to show his gratitude properly by returning the favor *'with interest.'*'' (Italics hers.)

De Mesa's (1987) analysis of *utang na loob* as a commitment to ''human solidarity'' is closer to the logic of Filipino behavior and Philippine language use:

> [*Utang na loob* functions] prior to any reception of favor.
> It is used as a plea prior to any favor because *utang na loob*,
> the debt owed to another person who shares a common human-
> ity (*loob*), exists just because we are fellow human beings.

The absurdity of the mercantile interpretation of *utang na loob* is embarrassingly humorous in a woman's "bargaining leverage" when in dire need of protection from physical abuse:

When that protection is neither forthcoming nor possible, she uses the only bargaining leverage she has left: a plea in the name of common humanity, a humanity that needs to be respected. She prefaces her request with *"Utang na loob!* Please, in the name of the humanity we share and the respect that you owe my humanity..." (de Mesa 1987)

Utang na loob is therefore a value which moves to recognize, respect, promote, and at times defend the basic dignity of each person.

Elevating the Status of *Pakikisama*

Of the three surface values, *pakikisama* (companionship/esteem) has received the most extensive treatment in the Western-oriented social science literature in the Philippines. It was used by Lynch (1961, 1973) as a primary basis for the construct of "smooth interpersonal relations" or SIR. Again the analysis suffered from the lack of attention to related concepts in Filipino. *Pakikisama* happens to be only one of the many levels of interpersonal relations in Filipino. In fact, the most valued form of relationship in the Philippines goes beyond *pakikisama*.

The construct of "smooth interpersonal relations" as proposed by Lynch (1964) is supposed to be acquired and perceived through *pakikisama*, using euphemism in the language and utilizing a go-between. He was successful in penetrating the highest level of interpersonal relations in the *ibang-tao* category, leading him to believe that *pakikisama* is a value. However, he did not take cognizance of the importance of the other levels of interpersonal relations beyond *pakikisama*, making his observation valid only to a certain point, and therefore inadequate. Lynch unwittingly reduced *kapwa* from the deep solidarity found in a shared inner self to superficial "smooth interpersonal relations." The inordinate attention given to *pakikisama* aggravates the unintended bigger problem identified by the historian, Renato Constantino (1970) in *Dissent and Counter-Consciousness* as the miseducation of the Filipino. He showed how the academician as "recipient of miseducation can very well be the Philippine society's mis-educator instead of professing the new consciousness."

Social scientists who unwittingly single out the concept of *pakikisama* from *pakikitungo*, *pakikibagay*, *pakikisalamuha*, *pakikipagpalagayang-loob* and *pakikiisa*, and then elevate it to a status of value is at the same time reinforcing (intentionally or unintentionally) skills and talents...sold to the highest bidder--usually the elite and vested interest groups. Without question, they reward docility, conformity and western orientation. The logical consequence is that they shrink away from social protest (Navarro 1974).

Pakikipagkapwa, not *pakikisama*, is what Filipinos value the most:

> More accurately, it is not *pakikisama* as value which is important but *pakikipagkapwa* as a Filipino *paninindigan*. Take the supposed social value of *pakikisama*. It is not even clear if one should accept and identify *pakikisama* as a Filipino value. If it is truly a value, how do we explain the fact that many insist on their *pagkatao* ("dignity") and *karapatan* ("right") *"ayaw kong makisama"* ("I don't want to conform"). Supposing one does not want to be part of corruption, he is identified as *hindi marunong makisama*. If he does not care for docility, conformity and the western orientation, he is *walang pakikisama*. What kind of value is that? What self-image does that create for the Filipino should social scientists perpetuate such an idea? It is probably understandable for a Westerner interested in Philippine society to jump to the conclusion that *pakikisama* is a Filipino value. After all, he is not immersed in the culture, his interests and goals are different, and he does not even understand the language! However, the Filipino should marshal his knowledge as a culture bearer and as a speaker of the language to heighten his awareness of Philippine social reality...The *barkada* ("peer group") would not be happy with the *walang pakisama* but Philippine society at large cannot accept the *walang kapwa tao*. *Pakikipagkapwa* is both a *paninindigan* (conviction) and a value. It includes all the other mentioned modes and levels of interaction. *Pakikisama* is a form of *pakikipagkapwa* but not the other way around. In fact, *pakikisalamuha* is even closer than *pakikisama* in meaning to *pakikipagkapwa* (Enriquez 1977).

While *pakikisama* is a comparatively high level of relationship, it is only so at the category of *ibang-tao* (not one of us). *Pakikisama* is only a building block among many in the development of a higher level of relationship. The other blocks include such concepts as *pakikipagpalagayang-loob* (level of mutual trust), and *pakikiisa* (fusion, oneness, and full trust). If all these building blocks are present, then the relationship can be said to have moved on to its highest plane, the category of *hindi ibang-tao* (one of us).

THE CONFRONTATIVE FILIPINO

The Filipino has been perceived in contradictory terms. Notable examples are debates on whether Filipinos are "basically gentle" or "violent" as a people. In Hawaii, Filipinos are characterized with both stereotypes (Ponce 1980). Similarly the Filipino is reportedly an "introvert" in one study but an "extrovert" in another. The concept of *frame of reference* should be given due attention as was done by Watanabe (1988) in his study of the Japanese way of perceiving Filipino characteristics in interpersonal relations.

Bahala na: Determination in the Face of Uncertainty

Among the first studies leading to the inculcation of *bahala na* as one of the Filipino's most important cultural values was that done by Lynn Bostrom (1968). Bostrom compared Filipino *bahala na* with American fatalism. She, wittingly or unwittingly, wrote that knowing the possible deeper meanings of *bahala na* is "not so significant as the fact that it is definitely an expression of fatalism." Fatalism here is being understood as a passive acceptance of the turns in the patterns of life, indicated by a dislike for planning and taking responsibility for one's actions.

Bostrom further asserted that *bahala na* "permeates the people's daily existence and influences their habitual activities. One's resignation to his fate is expected by other members of society." Bostrom again speculates that *bahala na* is an escapist value which "serves as a reliever of tension and a reaction against the social structure," and that it is "more strongly supported by society in the Philippines" and "may well be related to the fact that more of the country is rural" and lacking in (Western) education.

It was Osias (1940) who earlier expressed the more balanced view that *bahala na* is a combination of fatalism and determinism. He wrote, "It is expressive of courage and fortitude, a willingness to face difficulty and a willingness to accept the consequences..."

Lagmay (1976) has corrected some of the misconceptions about *bahala na* which gave the value, and to some degree the Filipino, a bad name. Firstly, Lagmay found that *bahala na* operates in a situation which is full of uncertainty and lack of information. The striking finding was that despite the uncertainty of the situation, very few would avoid or run away from the predicament. A person would instead utter "*bahala na*" and confront the situation. Therefore, contrary to the connotation of passive fatalism and escapism suggested by Bostrom, *bahala na* would be a confrontative attitude. It is risk-taking in the face of the proverbial cloud of uncertainty and the possibility of failure.

It is also an indication of an acceptance of the nature of things, including the inherent limitations of one's self. However, it is an acceptance which is not passive. It is as if one were being forced by the situation to act in his own capacity to change

The picture reflects the common interpretation of *bahala na*. However, research (Lagmay, 1977) shows the following characteristics of *bahala na*: (1) it stimulates action, not inaction; (2) it is not used in order to avoid or forget problems; (3) it implies perseverance and hardwork; (4) it gives a person *lakas ng loob* (courage) to see himself through hard times; (5) it stimulates creativity.

the present problematic condition. He is being required to be resourceful and, most importantly, creative, to make his situation better. Instead of the passive, expectant motivation often ascribed to the operation of *bahala na,* it is clear that *bahala na* operates to raise one's courage and determination.

Lagmay sees *bahala na* as arising from a social structure that spurs one to use his inherent abilities to bring about needed change, and that *bahala na* is a signal to be persistent in spite of the uncertainty of things. Furthermore, Lagmay states that *bahala na* reflects the improvisatory personality of the Filipino, allowing him to cope and be comfortable even in indefinite, unpredictable and stressful situations.

Lakas ng Loob: Inner Resource for Change

Coincident with the perpetuation of the accommodative and servile image of the Filipino, as portrayed by the supposed values of *hiya, utang na loob* and *pakikisama,* is the rash judgment that Filipinos lack *lakas ng loob.* If Filipinos don't fare as well as other nationalities in business, it is definitely not because of lack of *lakas ng loob.* It is unreasonable to assume the absence of guts and daring among a people who staged the first revolution against colonial domination in Asia. After all, Lapu-Lapu fought and defeated Ferdinand Magellan in spite of Magellan's superior arms.

Lakas ng loob is among the seven most highly-valued characteristics of the Filipinos found in a nationwide psychometric study of Filipino personality using the *Panukat ng Ugali at Pagkatao* (Enriquez and Guanzon 1983). With the Maranaos on top, the respondents from 12 ethnolinguistic groups scored high on *lakas ng loob* together with *pagkamatulungin* (helpfulness), *pagkamapagkumbaba* (humility), and *pagkamatiyaga* (perseverance).

Lakas ng loob is a key ingredient in the realization of *pagbabagong-dangal,* enabling one to face difficulty, even death, to vindicate the *dangal* (dignity/honor/ good) in one's being (de Mesa 1987). *Lakas ng loob* is a *damdamin* (internal feel/ attribute/trait) necessary for actualizing the good not only in one's self but also in one's fellow man (*kapwa*), in one's *loob,* and in facilitating the "social good" in *kapwa.*

The People's Power revolution illustrates *kapwa* and *lakas ng loob* as the businessmen and professionals from Makati joined ranks with the urban poor and protesting laborers from Tondo. The voice and *lakas ng loob* from Mendiola joined at E. de los Santos Avenue (EDSA) in a united move to bring about *pagbabagong-dangal.* Instead of the overdrawn and misused concept of *utang na loob,* the Filipino *lakas ng loob,* supported by his conviction and the social psychology of *kapwa,* was affirmed. The motivation to dislodge a dictator in the light of the values of *katarungan, kalayaan,* and ultimately *karangalan,* led to a demonstration of people's power in a move towards *pagbabagong-dangal.*

Pakikibaka: Cooperative Resistance

The dialectics of *kapwa* both as a psychology and as a world-view include not only *pakikisama*, as seen in the unity of man and nature, but also *pakikibaka* (level of fusion in a common struggle) in the face of injustice and exploitation. *Pakikibaka* as an aspect of a *kapwa*-oriented world-view awakens the Filipino's consciousness of present day realities and motivates him to be one in the struggle to break away from the clutches of the neo-colonial set-up. His motivation to struggle might be tempered with reluctance and doubt because the *kapwa* philosophy, is basically non-antagonistic. Elequin (1978) discovers this sentiment, reflected as perplexity in a *kapwa*-oriented world-view, in the song *Digmaan* (War) by Florante de Leon:

> *Laban sa kalooban ko man,*
> *Ako'y handang-handang lumaban*
> *Para sa ating kalayaan*
> *Ngunit bakit hindi ko maintindihan,*
> *Magkapwa-tao'y naglalaban...*

> (Though my conscience disagrees
> I am ready to do battle
> For the cause of our freedom
> But why can't I understand
> A struggle amongst *kapwa...*)

In a scenario where *pakikisama* is supposed to be the norm, *pakikibaka* is likely to be ignored as a value. First of all, if *pakikisama* is taken to be the motive for *pakikibaka*, that is, if one joins a struggle out of *pakikisama*, then the strength of will and determination implied in *pakikibaka* is not satisfied at all. It is also as if movements and struggles are merely social integration activities with no real higher ideal.

On the other hand, it could also be that *pakikibaka* is understood to run counter to the smooth interpersonal relations congruent to *pakikisama*. *Pakikisama* implies an adjusting of one's individuality (i.e., one's beliefs, principles, convictions, etc.) for the sake of some dubious social orientation. *Pakikibaka*, seen in the light of the corollary concept of *paninindigan*, can very well be a direct manifestation of *"di-pakikisama"* or *"ayaw makisama."*

However, if the normative value is of some higher form of interaction (i.e., *pakikipagkapwa*), a value which fully respects another person's being, *pakikibaka* becomes a valid and important value. *Pakikibaka* affirms one's convictions as part of one's being. It recognizes the meaning of cooperation and concerted action in resistance even when one is utterly powerless, which are aspects of the value of *pakikipagkapwa*.

The Filipino in the Third World is not all smiles and *pakikisama*. He knows the meaning of cooperation and concerted action to promote the rights of a minority culture. If *kapwa-tao* is challenged, the Filipino coping response is not *pakikisama* but *pakikibaka* even when he seems utterly powerless.

One must note that the Filipino does not always concede. He also knows how to resist knowing that *pakikibaka* (joining a struggle) is a valid aspect of *pakikipagkapwa* in the midst of inequality.

Table 5 gives an analytic framework of the indigenous Philippine value structure and correlated behavior patterns at the surface, core and societal levels.

In summary, Philippine values are classified into four major categories consisting of 1) surface values; 2) a pivot; 3) a core and 4) a foundation of human values. The four categories are placed in a system represented through a three-tiered structure with the surface on the top tier; the pivot and the core on the middle tier; and the foundation values on the bottom tier, with the pivotal interpersonal value *pakiramdam* underlying the surface, and the core anchored by way of the linking socio-cultural value of *kagandahang-loob* on the foundation below.

TABLE V

Behavior Patterns and Value Structure: Surface, Core and Societal		
Colonial/ Accommodative Surface Value	**hiya** (propriety/ dignity)	**utang na loob** (gratitude/ solidarity)	**pakikisama** (companionship/ esteem)
Associated Behavior Pattern	**biro** (joke)	**lambing** (sweetness)	**tampo** (affective disappointment)
Confrontative Surface Value	**bahala na** (determination)	**sama/lakas ng loob** (resentment/guts)	**pakikibaka** (resistance)
Pivotal Inter- personal Value	**Pakiramdam** *{Pakikipagkapwa-tao}* (shared inner perception)		
CORE VALUE	**KAPWA** (shared identity)	*{Pagkatao}*	
Linking Socio- personal Value	**Kagandahang-loob** *{Pagkamakatao}* (shared humanity)		
Associated Societal Values	**karangalan** (dignity)	**katarungan** (justice)	**kalayaan** (freedom)
Reductionist/ Functional Interpretation	"social acceptance"	"social equity"	"social mobility"

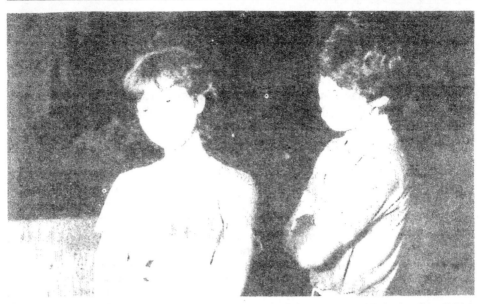

Tampo exists only when a relatively high degree of relationship is established or thought to be established. This could be found in the *Hindi Ibang Tao* category of level of interaction. *Tampo* can never be expressed to strangers. It can be directed only toward a member of the family, among friends, or to a loved one.

Tampo is a delicate feeling or behavior that is a result of not getting what a person wants from a person he loves. Daza (1976) found that *tampo* is temporary in nature. It is an activity that tests the strength or existence of a relationship.

The *surface* (on the top tier) is discussed by way of classifying the Filipino disposition as consisting of accommodative and confrontative *surface values*. The analysis of accommodative surface values includes a discussion of the inadequacy of the social interpretation of *hiya* (dignity); a critique of the Filipino self-image engendered by the supposed blessings of *utang na loob* (sense of solidarity); and the mistake of elevating the status of *pakikisama* (camaraderie) to a terminal value while *kapwa* (shared identity) is reduced to ''social acceptance.'' The analysis of the confrontative surface values which underlie the psychology behind the revolution of 1986 includes a phenomenological re-interpretation of *bahala na* (determination in the face of uncertainty); *lakas ng loob* (inner resource for change); and *pakikibaka* (resistance through cooperative action).

The *pivot* (on the upper part of the second tier) directly underlies the surface of the three-tiered structure. The pivotal interpersonal value, *pakiramdam* (shared inner perception), is explained and analyzed in terms of its behavioral centrality in the *biro-lambing-tampo* (tease-caress-resent) domain and in terms of the internality-externality dimension in *kapwa* psychology.

The *core* (on the lower part of the second tier) of the value system, otherwise referred to as *kapwa* psychology, is explained as an extended sense of identity. The concept of a shared inner self is given as a non-reductionistic alternative to the surface idea of ''smooth interpersonal relations.'' Reducing *pakikipagkapwa* to *pakikisama*, which also amounts to minimizing the sense of human solidarity to mere social acceptance and approval, is critically debunked as inconsistent with *kapwa* psychology and world-view.

The values of *kalayaan* (freedom), *karangalan* (dignity), and *katarungan* (justice) constitute the socio-political elements and foundation of the Philippine value system. *Kagandahang-loob* (shared inner nobility) is seen as basic/pivotal to all three.

Meanwhile, the constituents of the Filipino concept of social justice as a current rallying point in the Philippine value system are discussed in terms of/and in relation to 1) the distinction between law and the administration of law (*Wala sa batas, nasa pamamalakad ng batas*); 2) ''human rights'' (*karapatan*); 3) equity and fairness (beyond *pakikisama*); 4) ''truth and reason'' (*katotohanan* and *katwiran*); 5) justice as unity or consensus (*pakikiisa*); and 6) peace (*kapayapaan*).

6

THE DEVELOPMENT OF KNOWLEDGE
AND THE CULTURAL DIVIDE

The history of psychology as it has evolved in the First World can be interpreted as moving towards the goal of universality. As a discipline recently separated from philosophy and almost consciously modelling itself after the natural sciences, First World psychology has been partial to "universal" findings and the scientific values of replicability, verifiability, and "generalizability." In a sense, universality is the motive behind the series of systematically replicated experiments from rats to humans, from the laboratory to the field. American psychologists are no longer contented with white Anglo-Saxon sophomore university students. They are now equally interested in Blacks, Hispanics, and other minority groups. Filipino psychologists have gone beyond the convenience of captive university classes and air-conditioned Makati offices. They have gone to the field themselves. Just like their colleagues in anthropology and linguistics, the psychologist, Filipino or otherwise, would now occasionally face the discomfort of mud huts and mosquitoes. A researcher specializing in Maranao psychology once intimated that in the Southern Philippines, if the mosquitoes don't get the psychologist, the dissidents will. This development has its parallel in the international scene since more and more countries say "no" to cross-cultural researchers (Brislin 1977). However, while field research in Third World countries may not always be welcomed sociopolitically, it is probably a turning point in the growth of Western-oriented psychology since the data base of Western-oriented psychology is now much broader. It should be stressed, however, that a broader data base is far from adequate in assuring a global psychology unless alternative perspectives from non-western psychologies are put to use. In fact, there is a need to rewrite the history of psychology with due consideration for Asian thought, experience, and perspectives.

A Mercedez-Benz tricycle: Bridging the economic and cultural divide?

On the Dependency and Uni-National Dominance View in Psychology

A growing number of social scientists have been wary of the inappropriateness, or even patent inapplicability, of Western models in the Third World setting. It is ironic that most of the people expressing this particular concern are precisely the social scientists from the Third World countries who were trained in the West or in the Western tradition. Reservations range from a call to local adaptation or modification of Western models to outright charges of intellectual dependence and academic imperialism. However, some Third World social scientists acknowledge the problems but shrug them off on the ground that there are no suitable alternative indigenous models and concepts to use anyway. In addition, there are those who see no issue at all because they are convinced that any departure from the Western approach is blasphemy against the altar of science.

Issues along this line are not limited to Third World countries in relation to the West. It is also found in the West, as can be gleaned from Graumann's (1972) report as past president of the German Society of Psychology on the state of German psychology. He noted O'Connell's (1970) perception of "...a relatively uncritical dependence on American psychology" as "thriving in Germany today." Graumann found this hard to deny because "at least 50 percent (or even more like 80 percent) of all psychologists in the world live in the U.S.A. and a similarly high percentage of the more than 20,000 yearly psychological publications are written in English."

A similar observation can be made on the state of psychology in Japan as an economic giant and an Asian member of the First World, if not of the Western world, by affinity. Hoshino and Umemoto's (1986) report on Japanese psychology was indeed a description of the status of Western (particularly American) psychology in Japan. Except for localized exceptions such as the work on indigenous psychology in Kyoto, indigenous Japanese psychology is mainly handled by anthropologists, philosophers and humanists. However, as honorary "whites" in South Africa, the Japanese use Nihongo as the language of psychological science. Even selected articles from the popular monthly magazine *Psychology Today* get to be translated from English to Nihongo before they reach a Japanese audience.

Just the same, the American dominance view in psychology needs to be re-examined not only because of "the notable achievements of Soviet psychology which are relatively inaccessible mainly due to the language barrier" but also because of the invaluable resource lodged in otherwise ignored national psychologies, particularly from the Third World. Western psychologists themselves, who rally under the banner of "cross-cultural psychology," have pushed for a universal psychology, as contrasted with the psychology based on generalizations from studies done in industrialized countries. While the arguments are forceful and the sentiments real, a "cross-cultural psychology" will remain a promise for as long as the indigenous psychologies are untapped because of language and culture barriers. Of necessity, one must challenge the unstated bias in O'Connell's concern for the German dependence on American psychology and Graumann's measure for reacting to this concern. By "psychologist" they apparently mean someone who has an academic degree in psychology. A strict adherence to the union-card criterion for being a psychologist would, of course, exclude not only a sizeable number of eminent thinkers in the Western tradition, or people who happen to get their degrees in History or Anthropology in the specialized West, but also the unwritten but not less real psychologies of people who may not even have a tradition of publishing journal articles in psychology to speak of. The validity of unwritten psychologies does not depend on the extent and manner of their articulation.

Graumann's statistics on publications also imply a high regard, if not reverence, for the printed or written word. In this mode of thinking, one immediately looks away from cultures with unwritten languages and almost unconsciously looks up to the university-trained psychologist.

Research Approaches to the People's Psychology and Culture

Psychologists trained in the West rely heavily on the dominant, established research approaches to the study of psychology and culture. The research approaches commonly used are experimental research, survey research, participatory research and quite recently, indigenous research. Substantial differences can be noted among the four research approaches which can be traced, in turn, to differences in their respective norms and assumptions, distribution of power, problem definition, research design, data collection and utilization of findings, among others.

In terms of norms and assumptions as an aspect of informal culture, for instance, while experimental researchers strictly adhere to a pre-determined set of procedures, survey researchers conform to an informal agreement with respondents, participatory researchers negotiate issues jointly as they arise, and indigenous researchers seek to enhance awareness as one-with-the-other.

Distinctions can also be drawn regarding the distribution of power as exercised between researchers and participants in the various research approaches. In experimental research, experimenters wield virtually absolute power as they control the conditions, activities, and even the lives of their subjects in the name of scientific research. In survey research the researchers' powers diminish as they only define appropriate responses although they still decide the scope, locale and problem of the research. Further, the survey researcher is the arbiter on which population to study, even granting that the participants shall be decided within the limits of sampling procedures. The researchers' powers are further clipped in the case of participatory research wherein researchers and participants negotiate activities on equal footing; such powers are totally set aside in indigenous research wherein, instead of the researcher, it is the participant as culture-bearer who provides and determines the scope and limits of the research.

TABLE VI

A Comparison of Research Approaches in Culture Structure and Procedures

	Experimental Research	Survey Research	Participatory Research	Indigenous Research
INFORMAL CULTURE				
Values, Ideologies	Discover causal laws; internally valid experiments	Data-based relationships; external validity	Social change; relevant knowledge; mutual influence	Knowledge as praxis, consciousness, identity and involvement
Beliefs, Theories	Valid information from experimenter objectivity and control	Valid information from sample selection and statistical control	Valid information from relationships with research participants	Valid information from a multi-method, appropriate and total approach
Norms, Assumptions	Adhere to experimental procedure	Adhere to 'contract' with respondents	Negotiate issues jointly as they arise	Enhance awareness as one with-the-other
FORMAL STRUCTURE				
Division of Labor	'Experimenters' run 'subjects' in experiments	'Researchers' collect data from 'respondents'	'Researchers' and 'participants' work as colleagues	Researcher systematizes and participants reconfirm; researcher and researchee work at level of unity
Distribution of Power	Experimenters control subjects' activities	Researchers define appropriate responses	Researchers and participants negotiate activities on equal footing	Culture-bearer provides the implied and articulated limits of the research enterprise
TECHNOLOGICAL PROCEDURES				
Problem Definition	Experimenters deduce from theory	Researchers induce issues/variables from data	Parties negotiate shared interests and define problems	Problem definition given by the culture-bearer. Issues must be part of his awareness. Awareness may be created through involvement on the basis of identification with the indigenous
Research Design	From experimental design	From technologies for sample selection, instrument design	From pragmatic possibilities of situation	Research design as output and not as blueprint. Secondary research strategies (e.g. survey, experiments) adopted whenever appropriate
Data Collection	Run experiments and tabulate responses	Administer interview, questionnaire	Most credible party collects	Involved party collects. Quality of data as a function of critical involvement
Utilization of Findings	Disseminated to other experimenters for theory-building	Disseminated to researchers or policy-makers	Shared with others relevant to action	Primarily for the culture-bearer; not shared with others at his expense

Overview of indigenous research (Enriquez 1986). Statements on Experimental, Survey and Participatory Researches are from "Organizing Participatory Research: Interfaces for Joint Inquiry and Organization Change" (Dave Brown, *Journal of Occupational Behavior*, January 1983, Vol. 4 No. 1, pp. 9-19).

In terms of problem definition, experimental research on the study of psychology and culture is conservative in its orientation as it merely deduces from theory while survey research at least attempts to evaluate issues from data. Participatory researchers are even more liberal because in this research approach the researchers and culture-bearers negotiate shared interests and define problems together. The indigenous researchers, in an unprecedented move, go even a step further than the participatory researchers, thus in direct contrast to experimental researchers. It is the community of culture-bearers, not the experimenters, who define the problems and issues in this particular research method.

Research approaches in the study of psychology and culture also vary in data collection procedure. Experimental researchers run experiments and tabulate responses, survey researchers administer interviews and use questionnaires while in participatory research only the most credible party collects data. In indigenous research, on the other hand, only the involved party collects data, underscoring the importance of the people's critical involvement in indigenous research absent in the more established research approaches like experimental research and survey research.

In terms of utilization of findings, the experimental researchers disseminate their findings to other experimenters for the purpose of theory-building while survey researchers disseminate their findings to researchers or policy-makers to serve as basis or guideline for policy formulation. Participatory researchers, for their part, share their findings with the community involved and other institutions concerned with the research issue; indigenous researchers, on the other hand, use the findings for the culture-bearers' self-determined interests, never sharing them with others if doing so will be at the culture bearers' expense.

From the foregoing discussion, it can be discerned that while the researchers' powers and discretion are formidable in the established research methods to the study of psychology and culture, these powers are considerably pared down, and altogether set aside, in the more recent approaches like participatory research and indigenous research, respectively. Further, all these reflect the new thrust in social science research which gives increasing importance to the role and welfare of the culture-bearer. This is in sharp contrast to dominant research approaches wherein the social scientist totally controls the research enterprise without due regard to the special needs and cultural demands of an equally important participant in the research, the culture-bearer.

While there is a wide gap in the role, status and power of the researcher and the subject in the dominant research approaches, it is not the case with respect to participatory and indigenous research. This is because in participatory research the power and status of the participants have grown to those of a co-equal while in indigenous research the participant has finally become the power wielder, with the researcher relegated to the position of a research facilitator and consultant.

In indigenous research both the researcher and the participant can, in fact, be culture-bearers. It is therefore not surprising that the researcher in indigenous research expresses deep concern for the participant, both of them sharing the same cultural predicament, views and experience.

Further, experimental and survey research are sometimes used to preserve the interests of the powers-that-be and the social science establishment who wield a monopoly of power in the control and production of social science knowledge. The establishment social scientists can therefore be considered "research emperors" in their use of social experiments and surveys to perpetuate their own interests and to preserve the status quo, sometimes at the expense of the powerless indigenous people.

The role and power of the researcher in indigenous research, however, have been considerably lessened. This is because in indigenous research it is the culture-bearer, not the researcher, who defines the limits and scope of the research, relegating the role of the social scientist to that of a "research facilitator." Hence, the empowerment of the culture-bearer in indigenous research, a sharp departure from his powerless position in experimental and survey research approaches.

"Indigenization from Within" as Basic to the Cross-Indigenous Method

From the discussion of the various research approaches, it is apparent that there is a need to give due importance to indigenous research approaches or methods in the study of psychology and culture. The development and utilization of indigenous viewpoints can no doubt be approached in a number of ways. More importantly, it occurs at many levels and cuts across many disciplines. What appears to be an isolated development in a particular discipline in a particular country usually proves to be part of an over-all pattern. This observation applies with greater impact in Third World countries where disciplinal lines are not really as sacred as they are in the West.

An example of a possible approach to *"indigenization from within"* is outlined in Figure 1. To be sure, there are many ways by which this *"indigenization"* can occur. It may also be implemented as a policy (or as a strategy, depending upon native commitment to the idea) in a variety of ways. What seems to be workable in one Third World culture is not necessarily effective or workable in another.

FIGURE 1

Indigenization According to Source and Direction of Culture Flow

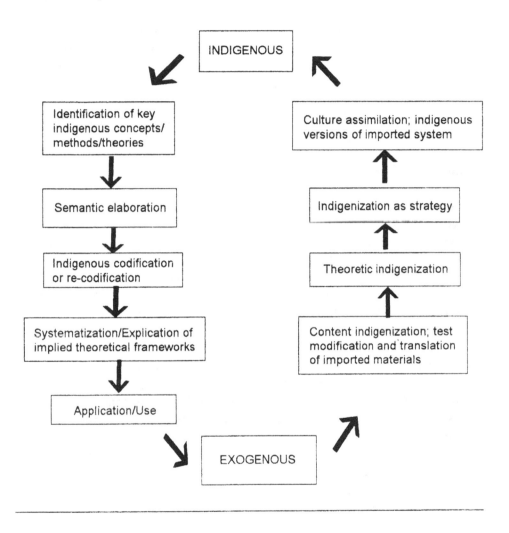

INDIGENOUS

Identification of key indigenous concepts/ methods/theories

Semantic elaboration

Indigenous codification or re-codification

Systematization/Explication of implied theoretical frameworks

Application/Use

Culture assimilation; indigenous versions of imported system

Indigenization as strategy

Theoretic indigenization

Content indigenization; test modification and translation of imported materials

EXOGENOUS

Comparison with other methods, techniques, etc.

Transfer of technology; modernization

Indigenization From Within
Basis: the indigenous
Direction: Outwards
(Culture-as-source)

Indigenization From Without
Basis: the exogenous
Direction: Inwards
(Culture-as-target)

It is easy to see that a number of approaches can be developed. Identification of key concepts followed by semantic and lexical elaboration need not be an element of *indigenization from within* in every discipline or country. What is essential are the source and direction of culture flow. Figure 1 schematically shows the contrast between an example of indigenization from within and without. The perspectives motivating either type of indigenization can even be working at cross-purposes. In fact, the term "indigenization from within" can be viewed as semantically anomalous. The term is proposed only as a convenient tool in the task of showing the difference between 1) the development of Third World cultures in their own terms as a natural process, and 2) "indigenization" as seen by people who habitually perceive the Third World countries as recipients and targets of culture flow.

Philosophical Issues in Indigenous Psychology

The notion of cultural validation is preferable not only because it moves us away from the political undertones of the term "indigenization," but also because it leads us to even more fundamental human issues. In the area of cross-cultural psychology, Serpell (1977) poses the issue as "revolving around *appropriate* ways of describing and explaining the behavior of human beings" (emphasis added). It can be argued that this use of the word "appropriate" advisedly takes the issue out of the exclusive arena of psychological and scientific disputations and puts it back where it belongs, i.e., the philosophy of values.

Figure 2 suggests a model towards global psychology through a cross-indigenous perspective. In this model, the different cultures of the world are tapped as sources of cultural knowledge. The resulting pool may then be called "cross-cultural" knowledge. More aptly, it is cross-indigenous knowledge, to distinguish it from the kind of "cross-cultural" knowledge derived from an application of the psychology of industrialized countries to data gathered from the Third World (See Figure 3).

Social scientists now find more time and reason (cross-cultural research is one) to visit the Third World. Castillo (1968) identified several types of visiting researchers sometimes fondly referred to by banter-happy Filipinos as "buisiting" researchers, from the "data-exporter" to the "penny-collaborator" and "professional overseas researcher":

> The "data exporter"...does research "safari style." He takes everything he can by way of data and leaves nothing of value to the country of his study. Sometimes he is called the "hit and run" researcher, with more "runs" than "hits"...
>
> The "hypothesis-tester" and "theory builder" has some theory as to how development proceeds, and his aim in overseas research is to add as many cultures or societies to his sample as he can to arrive at a universal generalization.

FIGURE 2

Towards a Global Psychology Through a Cross-Indigenous Perspective

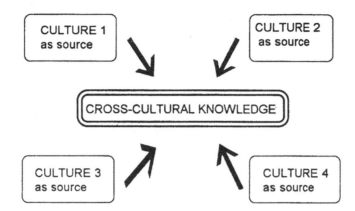

Note: The direction of arrows indicates "indigenization from within."

FIGURE 3

A Schematic Diagram of Uni-National Dominance in Psychology (Indigenization from Without)

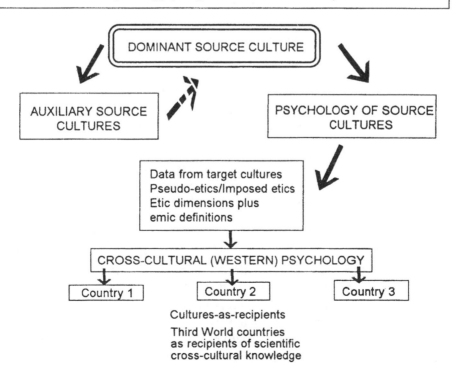

The "institution builder" is very organization-minded. He has a weakness for the creation of departments, institutes, centers, etc., if natives only knew how to put up project proposals. He is...a professional "allocator" of development funds, research and otherwise.

The "idea-stimulator" and "research facilitator" is a real gem. Professionally secure and very competent, he has no great compulsion to see his byline. He asks the right questions so that we may figure out for ourselves what the right answers might be; he assists in obtaining research support so that these answers might be forthcoming. Most of all, the research project is ours, not his. The only flaw of this precious gem is that he is such a rare specimen.

The "penny collaborator" happens to have access to some money, not too much but some. "How about a cooperative project?" he says. "I'll provide the money and you do the study."

To the "professional overseas researcher," overseas research is a way of life. He lives from research grant to research grant. "Tough life," he says, "I can't stand the winters of New York anymore."

Also included in Castillo's list of "buisiting researchers" are the "greenhorn," the "area expert," the "international development VIP," the "CIA scholar," the "instant expert," and the "research reviewer and critic."

"Buisiting" comes from the Tagalog word *buisit* (nuisance) with the English morpheme "-ing." Forman (1973) culled a good number of comparable examples on language mixing in a Filipino radio program in Hawaii. Contrary to the belief of some "linguists," *buisit* has nothing to do with "bullshit." However, this interpretation might yet come down as another example of "linguistic borrowing" in the Philippines, accepted simply because a lot of people thought it to be so, e.g., the Tagalog *"Kamusta ka"* as coming from the Spanish *"Como esta usted?"* In fact, the linguist Chan-Yap (1973) reports that *buisit* was derived from Hookien Chinese.

Brislin and Holwill's (1977) move towards increased cross- cultural understanding, in their study of the insider's view of reactions to the writings of visiting scholars, is not only suggestive in "the task of mediating between cultures" but also provocative as a step towards a cross-indigenous perspective. A tactical problem and advantage in Brislin and Holwill's study lie in the fact that the investigators themselves are not culture-bearers. It is not altogether easy to crack the emic barrier. This is probably the reason why Harris (1976) confused relativism with solipsism through reasoning by association in his article which purportedly discusses the history and significance of the emic-etic distinction. He is successful in further muddling the emic-etic distinction by associating the concepts with issues between idealism and materialism. Be that as it may, the problem with the emic-etic distinction can be partially traced to the ambiguity of the terms themselves (cf. Jahoda 1976a) and the apparent reversal of foci of meaning after the terms were borrowed from linguistics. Semantic controversies are notorious for eating up more time, paper, and ink than necessary.

Brislin and Holwill's (1977) warning against what they call "false etics" goes beyond semantics. The same holds true with Triandis' (1972) caution on "pseudo-etics." Unfortunately, "going emic" on somebody else's "emic" is painfully difficult. It is no different from playing the role of informant without being a culture-bearer. For which reason, one can look at an "imposed etic" as the strong version while the "etic-dimension-plus-emic-definitions approach" serves as the weak version of the pseudo-etic method.

The etic-emic construct covers a lot of ground both across disciplines (which Brislin 1976 sees as an advantage), levels, and extent of explanation (which Serpell 1977 sees as possibly leading to "over-elastic explanation") as well as across components or conceptually related or associated dimensions. We have the indigenous/exogenous, insider/outsider, particularistic/ universalistic, culture-as-target/ culture-as-source, and context-bound/context-free.

To this can be added the salient issues involved in distinguishing the locally codified topic from the locally unlexicalized topic and the related issue of translatable-untranslatable. We also have further refinements within the component dimensions, such as insider's view/outsider's view, insider-as-informant/ insider-as-collaborator, with the attendant issues of objectivity, distance, and the informant-as-misinformant (Bilmes 1973) vs. the informant as co-author (admittedly, these are two extremes).

Furthermore, we have usages in oral discourse (a reality which looms large in language use) which actually refers to the common-exotic and the transparent-opaque (as can be seen in the comment "if we don't understand something, it's emic"). Even ploughing through Pike's (1967) work would not help much in delimiting the extension of the construct. After all, nobody can legislate language use, not even with the guidance of language planners. It can be readily seen that it is quite a job explaining the meanings of the above-mentioned dimensions, not to mention the equally important job of discussing the theoretical linkages among them.

Rationale for the Indigenous Method

The indigenous method is of course motivated by the search for universals. As Jacob and Jacob (1977) in another but similarly motivated context put it,

> ...the variables affecting human relations may differ radically
> across national cultures, so that studies within one country will

not provide adequate evidence for universal generalizations
about social dynamics. At least one cannot tell without conducting comparative studies in a number of differing cultural
situations.

The crux of the matter lies in one's concept of a comparative study. The Jacobs
argue that "common tools and techniques are essential for successful comparative
research, and they must be relevant to the circumstances being investigated."
However, such tools and techniques have to be identified and refined. Even the
"simple" task of asking questions can have a variety of parameters to make its use
in one situation in the same culture different from its use in another, more so if you have
a number of cultural settings involved. Even assuming that the questions are "the
same" (after a series of translations, backtranslations, calibration according to
functional equivalence, contextualization, etc.), the answers may lend themselves to
a variety of interpretations (See Rubin 1976; Torres 1973).

While people find it easy to appreciate indigenous concepts (this is by no means
a closed issue, cf. A. Bonifacio 1976), they show initial puzzlement when the "radical
cultural relativist" tells them about indigenous methods. It is extremely hard to
liberate one's self from ethnocentric bias especially when "your way" has been
adopted and used in many situations and places in the world. In any case, it can be
reasonably argued that simply because the questionnaire has evolved into a technology
or even an industry in the United States of America, it does not follow that it should
be used in the Third World. Simply because the interview has been tossed about and
refined (in certain particular ways) in the West (from research to therapy), does not
mean that the Third World researcher and therapist should learn to do it the Western
way. (See for example Feliciano 1965; de Vera, Montano, and Angeles 1975; de
Peralta and Racelis 1974; Santiago 1975). Phillips (1973) was not even raising the
secondary question of appropriateness and applicability in other cultures in his book
Abandoning Method, where he challenged the use of interviews and questionnaires in
sociological research. He called attention to the more basic questions of validity and
data accuracy.

Jacob and Jacob (1977) see that "too much of social science is guilty of
influential propositions." To this can be added the use of influential Western methods.
Such wholesale use is sometimes tempered by token modifications but nonetheless
genuine interest in reliability and validity. In any case, little is heard of or written about
the issues of appropriateness and wastefulness! Researchers actually go to the farm
or to the mountains with questionnaires in a language the people do not truly
comprehend, even granting that the language is considered official in the country of
research. It is one thing to use English or French as a tourist but another to use it as
a researcher for one's Ph.D. dissertation.

The cost of research is a particularly salient consideration in poor countries. Some approaches can be very expensive by Third World standards and should be carefully weighed in terms of relative efficiency versus cost and immediacy of need. If the results can wait another year, it might even be practical from the point of view of resource training and institution building not to rely heavily on machines. The Third World's strength is in its people.

Instead of arguing about the relative merits of influential methods, the cross-indigenous perspective may be viewed in the light of Lagmay's (1984) total approach and Campbell and Fiske's (1964) argument for the multi-method approach. The cross-indigenous method is a call for the multi-language/multi-culture approach based on indigenous viewpoints (Enriquez 1975). Even if it is granted that the use of a foreign language and culture do not distort social reality in the indigenous culture, it still makes a great deal of sense for scientific and not maudlin reasons to use the local languages and cultures as sources for theory, method and praxis. As Alfonso (1977) puts it, the exclusive use of a supposedly international language "can lead to the neglect of the wealth of indigenous concepts and methods embodied in a language more meaningful to the culture." She contended that "developing and following a Filipino orientation in the conduct of research and teaching in psychology is not inconsistent with the goals of psychology as a science in search for universalities but rather a contribution to it." In fact, the cross-indigenous method better assures generalizability of findings precisely because several languages and cultures are used as sources and bases. The findings of Western-based psychology, as applied in research and practice in a Third World country using a Western language and orientation, can very well be an artifact of the language and the method. As a science, *sikolohiyang Pilipino* need not be caught in the debate between the nomothetic and the ideographic. It is not even a choice between the nomological and the hermeneutic. It is enough to realize that science is not value-free and that culture is a context for the scientific enterprise. Indigenous psychology does not aim to create a psychology applicable only to the indigenous culture. More accurately, indigenous psychology aims to develop a psychology *based* on and *responsive* to the indigenous culture and realities.

The Development of *Sikolohiyang Pilipino* Knowledge

In his analysis of the philosophical bases of *sikolohiyang Pilipino*, San Buenaventura (1983) identified three major goals of *sikolohiyang Pilipino*, which he called its *kaganapan* or realization, fulfillment, and completeness. These are *pagsasakatutubo* (indigenization), *pagka-agham* (science), and *pagkapilipino* (appropriateness to the Filipino/Filipino identity).

Steven Rood (1985) sees the "project" of *sikolohiyang Pilipino* as three interrelated tasks: the development of indigenous psychological concepts, the utilization of indigenous research methods, and the creation of a more authentic and appropriate social scientific psychology. Suspecting a bias for the Hempelian view, Rood warns against the "illusory search for lawlike generalizations." The cross-indigenous method seen in this light can profit much from such a warning but one need not assume that a dialogue between hermeneutics and empiricism is impossible (Meichenbaum 1988, Wakefield 1988).

National Scientist Alfredo V. Lagmay was clear in his stand that *sikolohiyang Pilipino* shall evolve on the basis of a "total approach." Lagmay was actually describing more than just a social science method, more than just a philosophical approach to *sikolohiyang Pilipino*. By *total* he was referring to the fact that while the method is objective and the bias scientific, the approach undeniably involves the total human being, including human judgment and human values.

To document *sikolohiyang Pilipino* values, ideas and activities, the poet Richie Valencia served as chronicler in verse. Not only did she write a narrative poem to record the proceedings of a *Sikolohiyang Pilipino* conference; Valencia also published a poem on the total approach entitled "Mga Tanong sa Syota Kong Engineer" ("Questions for my Engineer Boyfriend").

>*...engineer ka nga, ngunit ano pa'ng alam mo?*
>*engineer ka nga, para kanino ang alam mo?*

>(yes, you are an engineer, but what else do you know?
>indeed, you are an engineer, but for whom is what you know?)

>*kay galing mong mambalasa ng numero*
>*tumuldok sa calculator*
>*gumuhit ng libo-libong diagram*
>*at ilan pang kahig-tukang*
>*di ko mawawaan;*
>*ligtas nga ba sa sakuna ang plantang nuklear sa Bataan?*
>*ba't di mo alam?*
>*dapat bang bahain ang lupain ng Kalinga*
>*sa pagtatayo ng dam na di nila pakinabang?*
>*bakit di mo alam?*

>(you're great with numbers
>and fiddling with the calculator
>you draw thousands of diagrams
>and hundreds of scribbles
>i cannot possibly understand;
>do tell, are we safe
>from the Bataan nuclear plant?
>how come you don't know?

should we flood the sacred Kalinga land
to build a dam useless to the Kalinga people?
how come you don't know?)

marunong ka raw magkumpuni ng kotse.
sang-ayon ka ba sa Free Trade Zone?
sang-ayon ka ba kung tayong Pilipino'y
tagagawa lang ng bumper habambuhay?
marunong ka raw magtayo ng tulay,
ito ba ang diwa ng tinatawag na ''development''?
alam mo ba kung bakit laging baha sa Maynila?
tag-ulan na naman; noong isang taon,
binuksan nila ang mga dam
at daang buhay ang nawasak;
dapat bang gawin ulit ito ngayon?
makatarungan bang ginawa nila ito noon?
bakit di mo alam?...

(you can fix cars, so they say.
do you favor the creation of a Free Trade Zone?
do you accept that Filipinos
should make bumpers forever?
you can build bridges, so they say,
is this what they mean by ''development''?
can you explain why Manila always gets flooded?
rain has come again; last year,
they unleashed the dam waters
at the cost of hundreds of lives;
shall we do it again?
was it just, then?
how come you don't know?)

kay sarap pakinggan, kaysarap mangarap
subalit marami pa akong di maintindihan:
bakit puro dayuhan ang may-ari ng mga minahan?
alam mo ba?
bakit puro repackaging at assembly plant lamang
ang mga pabrika sa South Superhighway?
alam mo ba?
sa ilang malaking kumpanya raw,
mas mataas ang suweldo ng inhinyerong Hapon

> *maski marunong ang mga Pilipino,*
> *dapat ba?*
> *sabi nila mahalaga ang technology transfer*
> *para sa ikasusulong ng bansa,*
> *tama nga ba?*
> *tumaas muli ang presyo ng langis,*
> *kasalanan daw ng OPEC, hindi Caltex*
> *totoo ba?...*
>
> (it is heaven to my ears, a heavenly dream
> but i have much more to understand:
> why do foreigners own our mining lands?
> do you know why?
> how come the factories in the South Superhighway
> are all repackaging and assembly plants?
> do you know why?
> Japanese engineers get more
> for a job the Filipino can do better,
> is that right?
> they say technology transfer
> is needed to make our land prosper?
> do you agree?
> oil prices went up once again,
> do we blame OPEC or should we stone Caltex?
> we must know the truth.)

Among other things, *sikolohiyang Pilipino's* approach meant a recognition of science as a tool but not a tool for the sake of science. Analogously, the engineer's knowledge or the technical ability to build a bridge is not an end in itself. The "total" approach also includes the question: For whom are you building the bridge?

The Indigenous Methods as a Shared Cultural Responsibility

Equally challenging was the development and application of local and therefore culturally meaningful innovative methods:

> *Pakapa-kapa* (literally "groping") as a field method (Santiago 1977) together with *pagtatanong-tanong* (literally "asking questions" or "questioning") (Gonzales 1980) was elaborated upon and put to use. Other culturally relevant research methods and techniques such as *pakikiramdam*

("shared sensitivities"), *pakikialam* ("concerned interference"), *pakikilahok* ("participation as one-with-the-others"),
pakikisangkot ("integral involvement"), and *pagdalaw-dalaw*
("casual but repeated visits") were utilized in social psychology and personality studies, Sevilla (1978) provides a well-
written and positive review of the first studies done with such
methods. As she points out in her article, a Filipino psychologist with Western orientation would have to completely reverse
his research style and framework in order to be able to utilize
these methods to their fullest. (Ventura 1980)

It is not enough for the *katutubong pamamaraan* (indigenous method) to
respond to the canons of science. The actual development and implementation of the
method should also be sensitive to the situation and needs of the Philippines as a Third
World country. The method should by all means be objective, but the approach cannot
otherwise be but *total*. Multiple operationism is a value but the pitfalls of reductionism
are not to be ignored. Beyond the objective are a number of subjective constraints
weighed against the imperatives of methodological objectivity. Filipino psychologists
have long known that methods can be objective, subjective, and even projective, but
they should always be appropriate. A *katutubong pamamaraan* or indigenous method
in the Philippine context is not just culturally sensitive and appropriate. It is also
people-oriented, above all considerations. The "collective indigenous method" was
developed by way of threshing out research problems, data collection, interpretation
and use of research findings through community dialogues. The myth of research
expertise as the monopoly of American-trained specialists was gradually eroded.

Judy Sevilla (1985) sees three main reasons militating against the use of
katutubong pamamaraan. First and foremost, "whether we like it or not," is what she
calls "the pervading bias toward the use of English as a medium of instruction and thus
as a medium of thinking," an observation she finds applicable not only to the
indigenous methods but also to *sikolohiyang Pilipino* as a whole:

> If the use of our native language--whether Filipino or the
> vernacular--is vital to the development of a genuine *sikolohiyang
> Pilipino*, then the prognosis for such a discipline may not be
> very bright, considering the selection processes involved in
> entering college... The bias toward English and against Fili-
> pino, while attributable to other reasons such as "basic"
> colonial mentality, works against the use of indigenous con-
> cepts, theoretical frameworks and methods in the social sci-
> ences, including psychology.

The second reason has to do with the question of "uniqueness." Somehow, "Filipino psychology" connotes a claim to "unique qualities" apart from "indigenousness." Never mind if *sikolohiyang Pilipino* explicitly disowns such a connotation as outside its intended scope of meaning. Sevilla, however, longs for the unique, perhaps as a mark of identity:

> Yes, the methods are common to our experience and culture as Filipino, but doesn't an indigenous method go beyond this to connote a unique quality? That it is a method arrived at only because of and within peculiar cultural circumstances?

Visibly disappointed on this score, Sevilla finds the *katutubong pamamaraan* as not even unique to psychology. She admits that these methods may sit well with the Filipino in contrast to the impersonal and structured Western data-gathering methods. However, the more she reviews the methods, "the more similar they become to the techniques of anthropologists' and sociologists' participant observation." Undaunted, Sevilla looks at the possibility of a Filipino social science, a goal which she shares with *sikolohiyang Pilipino*.

Slowly but surely, *sikolohiyang Pilipino* contributes to the development of a Filipino social science. However, a third difficulty in the use and refinement of *katutubong pamamaraan* also cited by Sevilla has nothing to do with either undefined goals or insufficient motives. A truly debilitating cluster of reasons may conspire against *sikolóhiyang Pilipino*. Categorized by Sevilla as real world constraints, it includes lack of funds, a strict research schedule, the demands of specific funding agencies, and so on. However, in spite of her reminder on real world constraints, *sikolohiyang Pilipino* can still move towards its goals by simply riding on a strong drive to assert a shared heritage and tradition.

The Role of Documentation and Dissemination

Lack of funds, notwithstanding the determination, cooperation and concerted response of many people, has made the careful study and documentation of the social-psychological context of Filipino behavior possible so that, as Bonifacio (1980) puts it, "little by little, we shall be able to build a storehouse of usable information about our people." Information diffusion and literature exchange are central to the growth of the literature of *Sikolohiyang Pilipino*:

> Social science in the Philippines will not be effective in its attempts to understand and explain the way we behave as long as the indigenous sources of our actions are not fully docu-

mented [and] analyzed. It is only from such studies that a body of explanatory proposition can be generated. Unless we move towards this direction, with full commitment on our part, then we shall always be bound to Western explanations of our action and our efforts to contribute to hasten the development of our country will be very much less and the probability for us to be wrong will be much greater. (Bonifacio 1980)

Chided by a skeptic in 1976 that the accumulation of student research papers documenting varied aspects of Filipino psychology is doomed to be gnawed off by cockroaches in ten years' time, the *Sikolohiyang Pilipino* Resource Collection of the *Akademya ng Sikolohiyang Pilipino* was slowly but doggedly built until its 10,000th data paper on Filipino psychology, culture, history, and the arts was accessed and classified in 1986. Researchers from metropolitan Manila and overseas use the *Sikolohiyang Pilipino* Resource Collection, but they notice right away that this institution is different from other Philippine libraries. To begin with, all the forms are in Filipino, a practice which runs counter to the dominant assumption that English is the language of Philippine forms and documents. More importantly, the system of categorization, and thus the intellectual and conceptual organization of the resource collection, is in Filipino. Similarly, the records and index cards are in Filipino. Besides, the library users themselves directly help in building the library because they present copies of their work based on the *sikolohiyang Pilipino* materials they used. To top it all, the reading materials are written mainly in Filipino.

It might sound odd for a free country with its own heritage, language, and culture if it should turn out that the first and only library in Filipino throughout the Philippine archipelago is the *Sikolohiyang Pilipino* library. That is exactly the case as even the library collection of the *Surian ng Wikang Pambansa* (Institute of Philippine Languages) of the Republic of the Philippines is in English. A proponent of the National Language would hate to check for himself.

Much effort is exerted so that the extremely limited psychology materials in Malaysia, Thailand, Indonesia, China, and Japan are made available to the average Filipino reader who tends to be familiar with psychology in the United States only. For this reason, a compilation on *Sikolohiya sa Silangan: Pinagmulan at Patutunguhan (Psychology in the East: Source and Direction)* was edited by Layug, Ramilo-Cantiller and Esguerra (1987) and made available at the *Sikolohiyang Pilipino* Research Library and a number of university libraries in Manila.

The article on language in the 1987 Philippine Constitution definitely gave Filipino, the Philippine indigenous language, its rightful place vis-a-vis the colonial language. However, the Philippine postal authorities did not waste time in issuing a postage stamp on the Constitution in English. A new 100-peso bill was also promptly printed with the flag of the United States of America prominently displayed. The

American-oriented ruling class was not afraid of a nationalist backlash. After all, a group of Filipino teen-agers was asked by armed American soldiers to dance to the tune of the Philippine National Anthem and hardly an outcry was heard. Friendship and goodwill towards America was stronger than ever but a line must be drawn somewhere: the Philippine Commissioner of Immigration has ruled on mandatory AIDS testing for American servicemen assigned to Philippine bases, and the Philippine Senate has declared a nuclear-free Philippines.

Traditional Philippine Psychology and the Indigenous Historical Perspective

Historical consciousness and the appreciation of the value of documentation can only be heightened by the quick turn of events. The Philippine Historical Society and the *Pambansang Samahan sa Sikolohiyang Pilipino* joined hands in creating the *Pambansang Samahan sa Kasaysayan ng Sikolohiya* (National History of Psychology Association) in 1985. Historians and psychologists cooperate in the task of investigating the development of psychological thought and practice in the Philippines.

The exploration of Philippine psychology's usable past has proven to be essentially the same task as investigating the nature of contemporary indigenous psychology. Up to the present, the people who have quietly provided health and psychological services in the countryside are the *hilots, arbularyos* and *babaylans*. Somehow, the ancient practice of the *babaylans* did not turn to ashes together with the Batangas manuscripts burnt by the Jesuits in their zeal to supplant indigenous Philippine religion (Chirino 1604). The validity of a psychological theory, the utility of a technique, and the value of a manuscript do not depend on its form, be it ink marks on paper or etchings on bamboo.

The work of Filipino nationalist researchers on babaylanism gave the Archives of Philippine Psychology (which was established by constitutional mandate of the association) a meaning which goes beyond the accumulation of *sikolohiyang Pilipino* memorabilia. Souvenir items such as T-shirts, calendars and conference bags, historical documents and academic items such as drafts and manuscripts of papers and books, or even the carefully selected and enlarged pictures from the photograph and slide files of the archives, recede to the background beside a collection of *anting-antings* and panel displays on the indigenous diagnostic and healing techniques of the local *arbularyo*.

Still jubilant over the ousting of dictator Ferdinand Marcos, the *Pambansang Samahan sa Kasaysayan ng Sikolohiya* and the St. Scholastica Psychology Society, an organization of undergraduate psychology majors in a progressive Manila school, held a chain-cutting ceremony to open the 1986 *Araw ng Sikolohiyang Pilipino* documentary exhibit on the theme of Philippine resistance to domination. Aside from the ever-present yellow ribbon, the symbolic chain for the ceremony was actually an authentic memoir of "People's Power" eagerly cut in February 1986 from the barbed wires used to barricade Malacañang Palace.

The historians in the *Pambansang Samahan sa Sikolohiyang Pilipino* focused their work on local history and published them in Filipino. Under the leadership of Zeus Salazar, *BAKAS* or the *Bahay-Saliksikan ng Kasaysayan* (History Research House) launched a program of publishing historical works in the national language. Jaime Veneracion (1986) wrote on the history of Bulacan. Also written in Filipino is a study of Palawan done by Nilo S. Ocampo (1985). Aside from a series of local history publications, a textbook on Philippine History in Filipino under the editorship of Salazar is also underway.

BAKAS sponsors a series of history and psychology seminars, providing a venue for the critical assessment of the *sikolohiyang Pilipino* movement. In one of the *BAKAS* lectures, anthropologist Prospero Covar prompted a spate of soul-searching among Filipino psychologists when he charged that *sikolohiyang Pilipino* is firewood for the embers of American psychology in the Philippines. Ironically, the *sikolohiyang Pilipino* movement gets its share of criticism more often for being "Western" or not being genuinely "indigenous." Felipe Landa Jocano censured a study on Filipino creativity which aimed at developing a personality inventory and a psychological measure inspired by Mednick's Remote Associates Test. His main criticism: the method was too Western in orientation. Zeus Salazar offered a framework which places Jocano's sentiment on a level beyond a mere emotional outburst. Salazar distinguished the *pantayo* from the *pangkami* perspective, neatly highlighting the validity of Jocano's sentiment and Covar's perception of *sikolohiyang Pilipino* as fuel for American discourse.

Lagmay (1984) foresaw Covar's warning as a "basic difficulty." In his observation of Philippine research work which applies not only to *sikolohiyang Pilipino* research but also to Philippine social research in general, Lagmay called attention to the fact that almost all social science research work done in the Philippines was done by researchers and research participants educated in Western social science.

Salazar (1986) traced how the Filipino intellectuals from the upper side of the Great Cultural Divide, initially represented by the *ladinos* and the *ilustrados*, wrote their works with the Spaniards as audience. Later came the *pensionados* and then the Fulbrights, derisively called "halfbrights" by the outspoken philosopher Ricardo Pascual. Together with the Fulbrights, the Rockefeller and Ford Foundation scholars essentially wrote in the English language for their American audience. Concurrent with the Japanese rise to economic power are the growing number of Mombushos. The question is "will they be writing for the Japanese?" Part of the answer lies mainly in which language is used by scholars in the Philippines. In August 1988, President Corazon Aquino directed the Filipinos to use the Filipino language so as to eventually dislodge English as the language of government. However, English shall remain the language of Philippine scholarship for as long as the Filipino scholars who come back from advanced studies in Michigan or Yale choose to address the upper side of the Great Cultural Divide and write in the language of their alma mater instead of the language of the people.

Science and Superstition in the Corridors of Power and on Both Sides of the Cultural Divide

In a manner of speaking, the two sides of the Great Cultural Divide are initiating a program of "cultural exchange" as the native gets to be more and more interested in American psychology through the unlikely but decidedly powerful medium of the *komiks* (popular illustrated weekly magazines in Filipino) which now includes discussion of diverse psychological topics such as attitude change and the hierarchy of needs. Even the ever-popular concern with the nature of love has been dissected in the more sensitive topic of human sexuality. Filipino movies such as "Tagos ng Dugo," "Zapote Street," "Brutal," and "Biktima" graphically portray unusual psychological themes. Psychologists exchange views with listeners of popular radio programs where by way of sharing scientific knowledge, the myths such as the derivation of animal instincts from the drinking of cow's milk are debunked. What the psychologists might have missed in this "cultural exchange" is the fact that the supposedly untutored listener was actually talking in metaphors. He may not make sense to the Western-trained psychologist but they are both agreed on the rewards of breastfeeding.

For his part, the professional psychologist gets to be more and more interested in the popular mind even if his interest brings him to the study of the *manghuhula* (soothsayer). Estrada (1987) explains:

> The service of the *manghuhula* is availed of by practi-
> cally all levels of society although it has been observed   that
> the majority of the clientele are women. Although few women
> admit that they believe what they are told, the fact remains that
> they do see these soothsayers often on a regular basis. It can be
> argued that soothsaying is very deeply rooted in Asian culture
> and although Filipinos are very heavily influenced by the West,
> it is still part of that culture. It can also be viewed as a tension-
> reducing device because the seer who renders the service also
> functions as a counsellor. There is very little doubt that, verbal
> assertions to the contrary, many people order their lives or
> make decisions based on the prognostications of their personal
> soothsayer.

Soothsaying and the like are not the natural preserve of Asians. Former President Ronald Reagan of the United States of America was embarrassed by the revelation that his scheduling of decisions was influenced by the stars. Reportedly, his Filipino friends, the late President Ferdinand Marcos and his wife Imelda, were no different:

> The role of the *manghuhula* in Philippine society was brought into very sharp focus in the reign of the conjugal dictatorship. There is considerable evidence to show, for instance, that both Ferdinand and Imelda Marcos have their favorite soothsayers in the same manner that Hitler had a court astrologer who mapped out his destiny from time to time. Imelda Marcos seemed to have flirted with the occult not only by her use of the soothsayers but also with medieval necromancy, which is very interesting from a psychological point of view. In her bedroom in Malacañang, at the foot of her bed, a pentagram is painted on the floor. The pentagram is a traditional device of black magicians and necromancers in Europe. During the years that Imelda Marcos ruled the roost, the soothsayers acquired a certain *eclat* and prestige which perhaps, they may have lost since there is no evidence that the new President [Corazon Aquino] has any inclinations in that direction.

Reading tea leaves has an American version in reading coffee grounds; the *manghuhula* of Ferdinand and Imelda Marcos has a "sophisticated" counterpart in the astrologers of Ronald and Nancy Reagan. Many people look into the future by interpreting dreams, but few are born with the rare gift of seeing the future by looking into the coffee pot.

While the rich and mighty consult their private astrologer or soothsayer, the village poor sees a *tambalan*. Rebecca C. Tiston (1983) recognizes the role of the *tambalan* in dealing with disturbed social relationships. The *tambalan* follows "a prescribed pattern of folk diagnosis and culturally determined ritual," thus relieving suffering and reintegrating the individual client into the community. Tiston grants that the *tambalan* is a psychologist. He just happens to be "primitive."

The Great Cultural Divide separates the "primitive" *tambalan* from the "sophisticated" clinical psychologist. However, the two begin to unite as the people assert their cultural heritage and as the Western-trained clinical psychologist begins to appreciate his clients as Filipinos. Reporting on how Philippine clinical psychology has developed "the capacity to handle a wide range of client groups," apparently referring to the other side of the cultural divide, clinical practice has been characterized by Licuanan (1985) as moving "away from therapies that tend to be highly rational and verbal." She described Bulatao's practice:

> Using transpersonal therapy and altered states of
> consciousness, his approach to therapy is designed for the
> Filipino who is not verbal, who is more comfortable with
> concrete images rather than concepts, who respects an author-
> ity figure, who seeks group support and who is basically
> spiritual. (Licuanan 1985)

Such a practice illustrates a much-needed *indigenization from without*. However, clinical psychology is definitely isolated from the popular health sector and, to
date, is a failure in fulfilling cultural expectations. Exactly the same observation but
with reference to psychiatry instead of clinical psychology can be gleaned from
Higginbotham's (1984) case study findings on the mental health system of the
Philippines, Taiwan, and Thailand. Clinical Psychology must go beyond *indigenization
from without* and join the other side of the Cultural Divide by actually engaging in a
program of *indigenization from within*. The work of medical anthropologist Michael
L. Tan on the cultural construction of health, illness and medicine is valuable in this
direction (cf. Kleinman 1980, Kakar 1982). His scholarly interest in the indigenous
belief system is not limited to theories of illness causation reflected in the concepts of
engkanto (enchantment), *kulam*(sorcery), *aswang* (a creature which assumes different forms at night), *pasma* (sweating and slight shaking), and *hangin* (illness-causing
wind). He also documented the role of the *hilot* (local healer) as a health practitioner
who continues to serve the health needs of the people. Clinical psychology has a lot
to learn from the *hilot*.

Psychologists Danilo Bv. Tuazon and Alicia Salita pushed further the frontiers
of physiological psychology by exploring the physiological basis of concepts such as
hiyang (suited to one's health), *gigil* (suppressed anger or thrill) and *ngilo* (tingling
sensation). Likewise, Philippine psychopharmacology thrives on the rich lore of
medicinal plants (Concha 1980, Santos Flores and Tavera 1985, de Padua, Lugod and
Pancho 1977). One senses the excitement of rediscovery as psychology Professors
Violeta Bautista, Ma. Trinidad Crisanto and Grace Orteza motivate their students to
study indigenous concepts in psychopathology such as *mali-mali* (proneness to
mistakes/hysterical echolalia) and *bangungot* (nightmare) (Crisanto, et al. 1985).
Unlike clinical psychologists and anthropologists who outdo their Western counterparts by "still using the term 'primitive' to describe people of their own country,"
Tan (1987) incorporates social critique as well as advocacy in his studies.

A culturally sensitive health psychologist trained in *sikolohiyang Pilipino* is not
threatened by popular Philippine conceptions of disorder but actually makes use of
folk theories in his work with the people. He sees the *babaylan, arbularyo, hilot,* and
faith healer as his allies while his counterpart who styles himself a "scientific" clinical
psychologist rejects the *babaylan*. Higginbotham (1984) reported:

A scientific doctor is assumed to be inadequate if an illness is said to result from malign magic (sorcery) or an encounter with a malevolent spirit. The shaman or sorcerer is the correct expert, in the logic of barrio people, to resolve illness induced by man-eating spirit possession (*answang*) [sic], loss of soul, and taboo violation. Psychiatrists have little sympathy with indigenous explanations involving "devil possession." It is diagnostically termed "Follie a Familia"--delusional idea-tion shared among an entire family--and associated with lethal consequences... [A]ccusations fail to consider the substantial health contribution of community-sanctioned folk specialists (Lieban 1967, Shakman 1969) and, of course, the fact that barrio populations are out of contact with primary health care, let alone psychiatry.

According to Higginbotham, psychiatrists at the Philippine General Hospital (PGH) and the Philippine Mental Health Association (PMHA) respond to indigenous notions of psychopathology by teaching the Filipino family "to view the problem in psychiatric terms, 'educating' them to psychiatric methods." Even veteran profes-sionals look at indigenous health workers from a stance of superiority coupled with the judgmental notion that folk beliefs are "superstitious." They have the gall to tell their clients that "consulting a herbalist is just a waste of time." The village people naturally resist such claims:

Often, herbalists enjoy patients' trust, which remains to be won by psychiatrists. It was thought best to try to remain non-judgmental, although professionals usually asked their patients to try their therapy as an alternative and avoid seeing herbalists while under treatment. Generally, staff attitudes toward folk healers were that they interfere with proper care, confuse patients, and may cause more anxiety than they dispel. In essence, the accommodation strategy for handling clients with "unscientific" ideas is either to gently ignore them or persuade them to acquire an alternative conception--one that is more "psychological minded." (Higginbotham 1984)

It is indeed frustrating to realize that Western theories studied diligently are inapplicable to patients who hold folk conceptions. Filipino clinical psychologists had to be told by a seasoned Latin American therapist to recognize that knowledge of folk nosologies and culture-bound syndromes were useful in working effectively with traditional clients. For example, in the treatment of a Colombian case of "rainbow possession,'' a therapist was able to cure a catatonic patient by acknowledging the patient's belief in being possessed by the rainbow and by prescribing seven pills taken daily for each of the rainbow's seven colors. The patient was secure in the belief that as he secreted a different color of urine each day from red, orange, yellow and green to an even darker bluish color, the rainbow was being ''exorcised.''

While health service is actually delivered by the native healer, the Western-oriented clinical psychologist avoids involvement with the folk doctor. He views dealing with the *babaylan* as a waste of time and money, if not potentially harmful.

7

LIBERATION PSYCHOLOGY AND THE NATIONAL CULTURE

Providing day-to-day operational support for the liberation psychology movement, the Philippine Psychology Research and Training House (PPRTH) was established primarily as a research center in 1971. Reorganized in 1983 as a department of the *Akademya ng Sikolohiyang Pilipino* in response to the growing complexity of its activities which now include publications, a research library, a small bookstore, an extremely modest beginning of a museum, and short-term residence quarters for visiting researchers, the PPRTH plays a vital organizational role as national secretariat to organizations supportive of *sikolohiyang Pilipino*. The major thrust of the *Akademya* is to conduct studies on Filipino behavior and psychology, Filipino personality, Philippine languages, culture and history by using appropriate and culturally relevant theory and methodology. The *Akademya* facilitates the exchange of ideas through lectures by visiting writers and scientists. Social scientists from Asia and various parts of the world who are equally concerned with indigenous theories and methods took part in this forum of ideas. Durganand Sinha and Sagar Sharma of India, Fumio Watanabe and Takefumi Terada of Japan, David Ho and Geoffrey Blowers of Hongkong, and Navin Rai of Nepal were but some of them. The *Akademya* is not exclusively manned by psychologists. It includes historians, artists, and scientists in its staff, in the belief that the Filipino psyche is too important to be left in the hands of psychologists alone.

Aside from the Philippine Psychology Research and Training House *(Akademya ng Sikolohiyang Pilipino)*, a number of institutions and organizations foster *sikolohiyang Pilipino*. The institutions are the Bulacan Community Field Station, the Child Rehabilitation Center, the *Sentro sa Pag-aaral ng Relihiyon* (Center for the Study of Religion), *Bakas* or *Bahay-Saliksikan sa Kasaysayan* (History Research House), and the *Kasarinlan* (Independence).

Quonset House 1971

U.P. Alumni Center 1974

U.P. Faculty Center 1977

27 Matiwasay 1979

20-B Matiwasay 1981

5-B Marilag 1986-present

The Philippine Psychology Research House provides operational support to the
Sikolohiyang Pilipino movement

The organizations are the *Pambansang Samahan sa Sikolohiyang Pilipino* (National Association for Filipino Psychology), *Samahang Pilipino sa Sikolohiya ng Wika* (Philippine Society for the Psychology of Language), the *Pambansang Samahan sa Pagsasaling-Wika* (National Association for Language Translation), the *Pambansang Samahan sa Linggwistikang Pilipino* (National Association for Philippine Linguistics), the *Samahang Pilipino sa Sikolohiya ng Bata* (Child Psychology Association of the Philippines), *Buklod-Isip* or *Bukluran sa Sikolohiyang Pilipino*, and the *Pambansang Samahan sa Kasaysayan ng Sikolohiya* (National History of Psychology Association).

Established in 1975, the *Pambansang Samahan sa Sikolohiyang Pilipino* or PSSP is the most active national organization of psychology in the Philippines. It publishes its annual convention proceedings, a journal, and a quarterly newsletter. Its publications are in Filipino. The decision to use Filipino in an English-dominated Philippine educational system is of course a political decision. More pointedly, however, Rita D. Estrada (1987), a founding member of the PSSP, sees an "implicit political motive" behind the organized support for *sikolohiyang Pilipino*, "a hidden agenda," in her language. She explains:

> The oppression under the Marcos dictatorship was being felt more and more by [the] academe. The tyrant, in the short-sighted manner characteristic of tyrants, used techniques of thought control and censorship to still voices which were rising against his corrupt, brutal, and subservient rule. Any kind of voluntary and self-initiated grouping of people was suspect. The first of the freedoms immediately abrogated was that of assembly. However, a professional organization of academicians, it was felt, could exist without harassment as long as it stuck to safe topics. It could take advantage, however fragile, of the hypocritical assurances of the dictatorship that it would respect academic freedom. The founders had a hidden agenda-- the old spirit of subversion was very much alive. They felt that the organization, because it was strongly nationalistic, could reach out to our countrymen and that in the assertion of our independence as a people, the Marcos dictatorship could be undermined since it was fully supported by the American government in pursuit of their interests to the detriment of our country.

The PSSP explicitly states in its constitution the avowed purpose of developing active and scientific cooperation with similar organizations in the Philippines and abroad, with particular emphasis on Asia. The association aims to develop the use of psychology and related disciplines in applied settings such as education, medicine, agriculture, and industry. Finally, it aims to develop all aspects of the Filipino consciousness towards an active scientific and universal psychology.

The PSSP annual conferences have contributed to the generation and dissemination of the ongoing data-base on Filipino behavior. Conducted in Filipino, current issues and insights from various fields have further strengthened the direction of teaching and research in Filipino. Teachers in the behavioral sciences are assisted by the association in order to hone their skills. Members from various disciplines and various regions of the Philippines join hands in research, consequently strengthening links among the regions and facilitating intellectual discourse in the Filipino language. Although based in Manila, PSSP makes it a point to avoid "Manilacentrism." National conferences are intentionally held outside Manila not in order to bring Manila to the provinces but in order to learn from the wisdom of the regions and to profit from ethnic heterogeneity and consciousness. Concepts, data, and world-view are not exclusively drawn from Christianized Cebuanos or Muslim Maranaos. The indigenous perspective has brought *Sikolohiyang Pilipino* scholars to the Abenlens in the Zambales mountains and the T'bolis of Southern Cotobato.

Even the concept of a national conference, its culture, and practice can be an imperfect copy of the American Psychological Association's annual conference. Not so with the PSSP *Taunang Pambansang Kumperensya*. Consistent with the Filipino temperament, it has to have a *Gabi ng Talino* where young psychology instructors garbed in native costumes dance the traditional *singkil* in Los Baños, Laguna; where psychology professors and students sing of the good life in a free country, or perform in a protest play together with farmers in Muñoz, Nueva Ecija, shouting with clenched fists *"Ibagsak!"* ("Down with the dictatorship!"); or where a first taste of the Maranao way is experienced by the Christianized northerner as he has his dinner at the Marawi Conference.

The Call for Relevance

In his address as president-elect (1979-1980) of the *Pambansang Samahan sa Sikolohiyang Pilipino*, Manuel F. Bonifacio outlined a vision for Filipino Psychology by fully committing the association in the '80s "to pursue more vigorously the building up of local data in order to be able to contribute towards a better understanding of the Filipino and to contribute to the attainment of an adequate well-being for our people." He views relevance as a commitment to the understanding of Filipino behavior in terms of Philippine history and culture:

> One of the most critical issues facing [the] social sciences
> in a developing country like the Philippines today is the
> question of relevance. To us, relevance is not to be measured

only in terms of being against what is foreign and fully
endorsing whatever is national or indigenous. This kind of
stand is not acceptable because this is nothing more than gross
parochialism. To us, relevance should also mean being committed to know and understand the dynamics of our behavior
and identifying and establishing the local resources of our
nation. Our entire history cannot be ignored. It has to be
examined in order to have a thorough understanding of our
actions. We behave the way we do because of our cultural
traditions. To us, therefore, to be considered relevant is to be
fully committed by being totally immersed in the dynamics of
our society as it has evolved through time...(Bonifacio 1980)

Indigenous Social Science and Academic Criticism

The Los Baños, Laguna National Conference of *Sikolohiyang Pilipino* on the
Filipino Youth in the Third World was held despite the unusually strong typhoon of
October 1978. In support of an underground psychology ready to challenge the values
and practices of mainstream Philippine social science, the *sikolohiyang Pilipino*
association chose a young female undergraduate student providentially named after
a Philippine goddess, Diwata, to deliver the keynote address. Points of contact and
perceived differences between what Villacorta (1980) classified as two crystallizing
ways of thinking, i.e., "indigenization from within" and "dependence theory," were
disentangled through straightforward questions of priority on identity and exploitation. The indigenous stance in "Filipinos, unite!" was not seen as at loggerheads with
the Marxist stance in the slogan "Workers of the world unite!" Not yet, anyway.
Years later, Ignas Kleden (1987) voiced his fear thus:

...the idea of social science indigenization among academics
can be politically exploited. Broadly speaking, indigenization
is an approach which, on the one hand, will not accept that
social science in the developing world is a mere duplication and
imitation of that in the advanced countries, and on the other,
holds that both theory and method for the social sciences should
build on the findings of the culture and social structure of the
country concerned. The problem is: how far can indigenization
be taken without it becoming a kind of intellectual parochialism? It is not impossible that uncritical indigenization of the
social sciences could provide the justification for an
indigenization of social criticism and social control which
would eventually narrow the scope of academic criticism itself.

Not exactly a baseless, free-floating uneasiness on the part of Kleden, for indeed, indigenization can be used as a front for anything from "transfer of appropriate technology" to "sentimental revivalism." In the same manner, the views of the First World on the Third World can masquerade as a "Third World orientation." A program of research and studies on the Third World has to guard against control and domination by the background assumptions and terms of discourse dictated by the First World literature on the Third World, especially if and when such literature is not understood and accepted by the Third World people whose experience and views it supposedly describes. Caution is needed when the very language of communication used is not the language of the people but the colonial language upgraded in status and prestige to an "international" language. For as long as social criticism is perceived as the monopoly of an elite group of local intellectuals who remain content with communicating with one another in a colonial language not understood by the people whose society they wish to transform, and for as long as the indigenous mind is implicitly seen as incapable of articulating his critical assessment of his society in accordance with his world-view and tradition, then a Third World studies program shall remain a conduit for the propagation of the external view of First World scholars on the Third World. Kleden is right for, indeed, exogenous indigenization can be inappropriate and naive while endogenous indigenization must avoid a sentimental attachment to the past and be critical of local as well as Western values and wary of external social control masquerading as "academic criticism."

Sikolohiyang Pangnayon: The Return to the Village and the Upland

Instead of beating the drums for "academic criticism," psychologists, social scientists, writers, and artists from Metropolitan Manila and Luzon boarded the M/V Cagayan de Oro of William Lines from Manila's North Harbor to tackle concrete problems of village development at the fifth *Sikolohiyang Pilipino* annual conference held in Tacloban, Leyte in October 1979. It was the first time ever that a national psychological convention was held outside Luzon and the Greater Manila area. The conference chairman, Leonardo Mercado, a Filipino Catholic priest who delivered his talk in Pilipino (as the national language was then spelled, with a P) at the First National Conference in Diliman in 1975, insisted on publishing the conference proceedings in English--a controversial move which eventually led to the formal inclusion of an article on language in the amended PSSP constitution mandating that all conferences, seminars, meetings, and official publications of the association shall be in the national language of the Philippines. Meanwhile, Antoon Postma, a Catholic priest from the Netherlands who came to the Philippines in 1957 and worked among the Mangyans of Mindoro a year after, won the admiration of the association. Postma delivered his paper in Pilipino, supporting the participants who resolved to use the native language in spite of the apparent change of heart on the part of the conference chairman who hosted the Tacloban conference as president of the Divine Word University.

Psychology outside the university: Using the Philippine Thematic Apperception Test (PTAT) in a remote Philippine barrio.

Psychological research and testing away from transnational corporation-oriented Makati.

A forester and social psychologist, Abraham Velasco led the association as fourth president from 1983-1984. His experience and training as forester put him out of place in the minds of elitist psychologists. He was actually asked to explain just what exactly a forester was doing in psychology, or more pointedly, what psychologists would do in the forest: "Psychologize the trees?" Thanks to Velasco, the answer to that question bolstered the argument for offering a course on field methods in pscyhology in the Philippine psychology curriculum. Third World psychology means serving the underserved. In the Philippines, it means going to the uplands.

At this point, Carl Jung's advice on avoiding the university if one wants to learn psychology becomes even more appropriate. But how can academic psychology ever avoid the university? One possible way is by getting out of the classroom, the psychology laboratory and clinic. This move, however, appeared too radical to conservative members of the psychology faculty at the University of the Philippines, who opposed the institution of a course on Field Methods in Psychology because the course had no precedent in an American university. But getting out of the classroom is not anything new in academic Philippine psychology. Sinforoso Padilla provoked the curiosity and interest of his psychology students in the 1930s by taking them to natural campus settings outside the classroom. He would intentionally dislodge a pen from its inkstand and scatter flowers from the vase on a table in the waiting room leading to his office and then ask his Filipino students to explain their *pakikialam* (concerned interference), for the students almost invariably straightened out the table for him. He would bring his students to the heart of crowded Manila in fashionable Escolta, and plant a few confederates to crowd around a spot on the sidewalk, thereby enticing more people to do the same, if only to prove the point that people are naturally curious. Padilla's students used to create an artificial fiesta atmosphere on Quiapo bridge as people observed the Pasig waters from the railings simply because there were enough people around doing the same. The students vividly remembered Professor Padilla more than four decades later.

Local travel was definitely a lot easier in the 1960s than the 1930s. During the 1960s, psychology students from Diliman were not confined to Metropolitan Manila. They went as far as Mt. Banahaw in Laguna or even Puerto Galera in Mindoro, using university-owned vessels such as the M/V Pampano. The call for an organized and systematic field approach to indigenous psychology underscored the need for a community base where psychologists can learn from the people and share what they have learned with them.

The Bulacan Community Field Station (BCFS) was established for the purpose of developing a practical site for community psychology. A field station in a rural area consisting of a bungalow with limited amenities, a furniture factory site, a couple of huts, and a water pump which sometimes worked, became available to psychology researchers in the 1960s as townsfolk migrated to Manila and the United States. The furniture factory was abandoned eventually as more and more workers opted to work in the Middle East. Though fast "urbanizing," BCFS served as a gateway to the uplands of Sierra Madre in Norzagaray, Bulacan and was formally organized by 1982 under the supervision of a board of directors consisting of farmers, local town leaders, and academics. Community dialogues and psychology classes were held under the mango trees or the blue sky, weather permitting. Professional and student researchers from the Pamantasan ng Lunsod ng Maynila, University of Santo Tomas, De La Salle University, Assumption College, and the University of the Philippines were re-oriented to the rural communities of Balagtas, Bulacan instead of drawing all their motivation for further advancement from transnational corporation-oriented Makati.

More importantly, service is extended whenever possible and called for. It is not enough for a psychologist of language to discover that community children have low recall for action verbs as compared with other words. The effort does not stop at writing a paper on language recall for the *sikolohiya ng wika* seminar. Research findings are discussed with interested parents and school teachers. A training exercise for the children is developed and implemented in the community in order to improve relevant recall performance. As a result of activities of this nature, a tangible basis for a *Sikolohiyang Pangnayon* (Rural Psychology) has emerged from the barrio experience.

Western-oriented psychology, as Durganand Sinha (1984) observed in his invitational address to the International Congress of Psychology in Acapulco, Mexico, was largely an "urban" discipline:

> ...dealing primarily with middle class and upper middle class population and with institutional problems stemming from urbanization and modernization. Only recently the focus has shifted to the poor, underprivileged and the blacks. In India, due to the paramount importance of the rural sector in our life and economy, it was but natural that psychologists concentrated on problems of rural development and agro-economic growth, poverty and deprivation.

Sinha could just as well have written about the Philippine situation. *Sikolohiyang Pilipino* is a move towards the development of rural psychology. Sinha's prediction that "rural psychology" is likely to develop in due course into a distinct branch of applied psychology is supported by the development of *sikolohiyang pangnayon* (village psychology) and the *katutubong pamamaraan* (indigenous method) in the Philippines.

Sikolohiyang Pangsining: Advocacy for People's Art and Psychology

The sense of freedom that goes with the realization that psychology need not be imported from the United States of America brought new vigor, new meanings, and new directions for Philippine psychology. An intriguing redefinition of psychology itself is foreseen with the Filipino psychologists' growing interest in the arts. Imbued with a dynamism and a commitment to indigenous Filipino psychology in music and the arts, Felipe de Leon, Jr. led the *sikolohiyang Pilipino* movement as fifth president of the association (1985-1986), promoting consciousness in people's art. De Leon (1981) distinguishes *people's art* from *specialist art*. The first includes traditional, indigenous, ethnic, and folk art. To be sure, people's art "exists everywhere in the country, especially among our rural and urban populations whose education is more or less synonymous with the life process in the community rather than with the artificially structured, essentially theoretical, mental learning that occurs in a formal setting such as a school. It is an art integrated in myriad ways with everyday concerns, interests, functions, and activities." *Specialist art*, on the other hand, "is the product of individuals whose minds are essentially molded in academic institutions such as a college of liberal arts or school of fine arts, literature, music, dance, drama, or film."

Apart from identifying the roots of *sikolohiyang Pilipino* in people's art as against the impact of *sikolohiyang Pilipino* on specialist art as it is transformed in the Philippine setting, nothing definitive has surfaced in Philippine academic psychology as yet. In fact, the resistance from American-oriented psychologists is so strong that people's art, particularly traditional Philippine art, began to have a place in courses like psychology of perception only in the '80s. *Sining Sikolohiyang Pilipino*, as an organizational venue for psychologists in the arts, was launched in 1983 as an offshoot of the Marawi Conference on the Filipino Personality and the Indigenous Arts. Drama, music, dance, and the visual arts lend a new excitement to psychologists as the artists exchange views with them. The unity of psychology and art in the people's culture becomes immediately apparent in daily human activities right in places where people live and work instead of at the Cultural Center, art galleries, museums, and concert halls required by *specialist art*:

> Putting a baby to sleep evokes a hauntingly beautiful lullaby from his mother. A childless couple praying for a son performs an exquisite dance in front of a church. A young man courting the prettiest maiden in town serenades her with a most lovely and tender melody. A *pasyon* play is performed and suddenly the whole barrio is transformed into a giant stage. The most practical objects of everyday life--chairs, tables, beds, mats, hats, combs, ornament, utensils, containers, bags, baskets, costumes, and many more--are at the same time endowed with aesthetic forms of the highest order. (de Leon 1981)

Folk art, as it reflects the concept of *kapwa*, is a rich source for understanding the Filipino world-view. Guillermo (1986) concluded that various forms of artistic expression, like the treatment of space in the Filipino house or its extensions, the jeeps, buses, and taxis, manifest the Filipino's need for company, shunning aloneness:

> Close family ties are seen in the indigenous house. In the standard nipa hut, which is the basic indigenous house with regional variations, there are no room partitions... The members of the family all sleep together in one room, often including other relatives and even guests. Little value is thus placed on individualism and privacy. (Guillermo 1986)

The openness as well as the present gradual development of mass-based artists whose aesthetic interests lie in depicting the peaks, depths, hardships, and aspirations of contemporary Filipino life undoubtedly touch on *pakikiisa*, the highest level of *kapwa* psychology.

De Leon formed a choral group called *Kasarinlan* (Independence) and initiated the annual *Kasarinlan* presentation advertised in programs as *anting-anting* (amulet). As he puts it, *sikolohiyang Pilipino* can be used as *anting-anting* to counter the undue influence of American culture. It is sad to admit that Philippine music is not heard over airlanes controlled by American recording companies. To hear and enjoy your own country's music for the first time as an adult is a beautiful experience. The Filipino had a chance to hear token samples of Philippine music from different ethnic groups such as *"Ati cu pong singsing"* from the Pampangos, *"Sarungbanggi"* from the Bicolanos, *"Ay, Ay Kalisud"* from the Visayas, and *"Pamulinawen"* from the Ilocos region, but that was just about it. The American-dominated recording industry would rather dish out Madonna's "Vogue" or the latest pop music from the United States or England. Performances by Kasarinlan make the Filipino aware of the great wealth of Philippine music. Besides, the performances raise funds for the *Sikolohiyang Pilipino* movement.

The relevance of social issues and Philippine life to literature in general and the short story in particular impelled Melendrez-Cruz (1986) to remind the Filipino writer that as a Filipino he has an obligation to respond to the people's needs and problems. The Filipino writer, once enchanted by the colonizer, unwittingly helped maintain the status quo as if under a spell. The *kapwa*-oriented world-view was displaced by an imported ideology in the guise of humanism, thus quelling the resistance against the existing socio-economic structure. As Cruz puts it, a truly Filipino world-view necessarily includes the realization that the Filipinos are the "true creators of their own destiny."

Valerio Nofuente (1978), who met a violent death under mysterious circumstances in 1981 and was subsequently honored as a martyr to the cause of the nationalist struggle, went a step further. Calling attention to radio and TV drama as powerful instruments in the shaping of a way of life, he was painfully aware that the media is vulnerable to manipulation by the powers-that-be. Through TV and radio drama, a distorted view of reality can be developed, conditioning people to become passive even in the face of blatant social ills of the country. Thus, the perception of ideological manipulation in an attempt to manufacture a new world-view, or a supposedly Filipino ideology, comes to the fore. For example, the notion that the "oppressed are blessed" is propagated through the mass media, encouraging the Filipino to be content with his lot and not strive for a better life. Helen Remonteza is a good example from Philippine drama:

> Helen Remonteza--a woman, ready to shed tears, get hurt, face life, and shoulder the world of sufferings. Helen Remonteza--will cry, hurt herself and sacrifice in the name of love...(Nofuente 1979)

There is no evidence whatsoever that suffering is a necessary ingredient of the Filipino world-view. The European concept of a suffering Christ has not captured the Filipino psyche. Even on Good Friday, the atmosphere around the *bisita* (makeshift chapel) is festive. The allure of the *Santo Niño* (Child Jesus) and of the triumphant Jesus of the *pasko ng pagkabuhay* (Easter Sunday) as celebrated in places like Balintawak, as against the crucified Christ, is so compelling one does not wonder why Filipinos refuse the image of a suffering Christ with a crown of thorns as guardian to the remains of their ancestors. Recognizing and starting out from his basically *kapwa* orientation is perhaps the Filipino's first step towards his liberation. Delineating the Filipino psychology and world-view is a contribution towards that end--by not simply describing the Filipino outlook as seen in his arts, in his behavior and culture, but in moving him to action on the basis of his own world-view and on his own terms.

Having artists in a psychology association has many meanings. In the practical organizational sense, it could mean having an attractive logotype for the association and colorful designs for the souvenir T-shirts announcing the annual conferences. It could also mean an *awit* and a hymn composed for the association. But who is to determine its deeper meanings? Perhaps the therapeutic and liberating characteristics of the creative process shall be delineated or perhaps the Asian soul shall be rediscovered. But more importantly, the surge of interest in the arts changes the self-image of the Filipino psychologists themselves, and perhaps even their identity. After all, it can be argued that psychologists must move closer to art not in order to avoid psychology but precisely in order to approach its very core.

Sikolohiyang Pangrelihiyon: Babaylanism and Philippine Religion

The task faced by *sikolohiyang Pilipino* is indeed awesome. Work on *babaylanism* has hardly begun and well-meaning people already dismiss the *babaylans* as mere "shamans." Work has to be done on many frontiers. Concepts such as "Folk

The healing tradition of the *babaylan* and *catalonan* lives on despite its long history of suppression and the promotion of "modern healing methods."

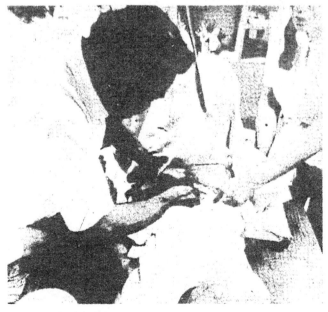

Faith healers are the modern descendants of the *babaylan* and *catalonan*. Their method of healing, which uses the concepts of *kaluluwa* and *ginhawa*, is effective because it is deeply rooted in the indigenous psyche.

Catholicism'' had been bandied about long enough for people not to realize that more accurately, the phenomenon to study and refer to is "Christian Anitism." Research on *Bathalismo* was still on the drawing boards of the *Sentro sa Pag-aaral ng Relihiyon* founded by Violeta Bautista in 1984. However, questions on the status of indigenous religion were already being raised. Scientific understanding and consciousness of Catholic Bathalism merit a very high priority in a Filipino-oriented psychology.

Meanwhile, the psychology of Islam in the Philippines is evaluated in terms of indigenous realities with the resulting emphasis on similarities instead of differences. Casiño (1973) highlighted ''a small detail and a bit of psychology'' by focusing on the question of Christian and Muslim names. He asks:

> Would it not be better if Christian and Muslim Filipinos considered the adoption of both spellings of Semitic names without regard to religious affiliation so that a Tagalog can be Jose or Yusuf, a Waray can be Maria or Miriam, a Maranao can be Abraham or Ibrahim, etc.? This would underline the commonality of our Semitic heritage of personal names...Few people have taken the trouble to point out that such names, though variously spelled, derive from a common source. The following is a partial list:

Eastern Spelling	Western Spelling
Hawa	Eve, Eva
Harun	Aaron
Nuh	Noah
Ibrahim	Abraham
Ishak	Isaac
Yakub	Jacob
Musa	Moses, Moises
Sulaiman	Solomon
Yahya	John, Juan
Yusuf	Jose, Joseph
Miriam	Mary, Maria
Gibrai'l	Gabriel
Isa	Jesus
Masi	Messiah
Nazrane	Nazarene

More accurately, "folk Islam" is Islamized animism. The choice is not between the crescent and the cross. The bone of contention is not even the psychology of "folk Islam" nor the identity of Filipino Muslims. In the eyes of psychologist Abdul Hamid al-Hashimi, the issue is on Islamizing the discipline of psychology:

> In psychology imitation was the rule...Our young men returned from the West and proudly repeated what they have learned, without distinguishing the worthwhile from the worthless. In many cases, they translated the books they had studied and used them as textbooks, unaware that the psychological situations and cases they were teaching to their students were French, English, American and Russian, not Muslim.

Bautista focused her initial efforts on the scientific study of Philippine morality and ethics and the indigenization of theology. Fortunately, de Mesa of the Maryhill School of Theology is on hand to help in the big task ahead with his insightful analysis of *loob* as shared humanity. Popular expressions such as "*Sapagkat kami'y tao lamang*" ("Because we are but human") and "*Ganyan lang ang buhay*" ("That's life") were used as points of departure in understanding the contemporary morality of the Filipino (Maningas 1984).

Dionisio Miranda (1987) of the Society of Divine Word provided valuable insight by showing the centrality of *pagkamakatao* as "virtue" in Filipino character and ethics:

> Surprisingly, *pagkatao* coincides with the concept of character in an essentialist, one could even say, ontological, sense. It is the state or mode of being human. To make it more explicitly moral, however, it might be better to speak of *asaltao* (human conduct) or more dynamically, *pagkamakatao*, being human in the sense of being, behaving, and relating in a human manner...*Pagkamakatao* can also be loosely translated as humaneness. That this concept is ultimately consonant with an ancient philosophical insight may be seen by comparing it with the meaning of the Latin *virtus*, which fundamentally means an essentially human quality, worth or moral excellence and only secondarily means manliness. (Miranda 1987)

Thanks to the *Sentro sa Pag-aaral ng Relihiyon* and the *Pambansang Samahan sa Kasaysayan ng Sikolohiya*, Philippine psychology in the tradition of Babaylanism finally got the attention it long deserved. The names of "Papa" Isio and Estrella Bangutbangwa were at long last heard in the same seminar halls that used to recognize only the venerable names of Sigmund Freud or Burrhus Frederick Skinner. *Anting-antings* were displayed in halls used to exhibit computers and teaching machines. But walls of prejudice do not come down easily. A coed from an exclusive school for the elite did not object to the historical and psychological interest given to Babaylanism and the respect accorded to Bangutbangwa. After all, the *babaylans* were at the forefront of social and national revolutions (Bauzon 1985, Cullamar 1986). The coed simply found Bangutbangwa's family name "baduy," a disparaging term used to characterize the unsophisticated ways of people from the other side of the Great Cultural Divide.

Sikolohiya ng Wika: National Consciousness and the Indigenous Language Movement

Even more noticeable than the role of the arts was the very important role the indigenous language played in the development and articulation of *sikolohiyang Pilipino*. The *Samahang Pilipino sa Sikolohiya ng Wika* or SPSW (Philippine Society for the Psychology of Language) was founded in 1971 to generate ideas and report empirical findings on the psychology of language. SPSW has been active with seminars held once or twice a year. It is from these seminars that student papers on the psychology of language and important theoretical papers on the *sikolohiyang Pilipino* perspective such as Salazar's (1981) analysis of affixation and *hiya* are presented and discussed prior to publication.

SPSW is now envisioned as an association likely to play an important role in the Philippine struggle against a colonial language. Based on a series of long-term studies, psychological tests, and surveys, Jasmin Acuña (SPSW president, 1986-1987), a cognitive psychologist who received her Ph.D. from the University of Chicago, published a book on language and cognition tracing the cognitive development of the Filipino child and showing the importance of the Filipino language versus English in the teaching of science (Acuña 1987). Science teaching in the Philippines is still primarily done in the colonial language. The language struggle was not a picnic from the beginning, but somehow, what appeared to be obstacles at first were in effect blessings to the movement. An administrator threatened to create a committee to investigate the teaching of psychology in Filipino, but instead of dampening spirits, his move spurred the publication of *Sikolinggwistikang Pilipino*, a collection of scientific studies on the psychology of the Filipino language written in Filipino (Enriquez 1976). The struggle for Filipino in psychology and the sciences goes on.

The link between national consciousness and language in Philippine psychology was subjected to a series of psychological studies which highlight the Filipino cultural struggle against the American neo-colonial hold on the Filipino people. Emphasis on the national language as a matter of cultural survival also helped in renewing the Philippines' cultural and linguistic ties with other Southeast Asian nations. Directions and developments in Bahasa Indonesia and Bahasa Malaysia are taken into account by psychologists of language in the *Samahang Pilipino sa Sikolohiya ng Wika* as the concept of Bahasa Filipino is fleshed out in discussions on spelling, semantics, and technical terminology. Psychologists seized the opportunity to develop the technical terminology of psychology in Filipino (Enriquez and Marcelino 1984). The active use of the Filipino language fostered the organization of professional translators. The *Pambansang Samahan sa Pagsasaling-Wika* was founded in 1983 by Lilia F. Antonio for the purpose of promoting the art of language translation. The *Pambansang Samahan sa Linggwistikang Pilipino*, a very active organization of linguists with a decidedly Philippine orientation, joined hands with the *Pambansang Samahan sa Sikolohiyang Pilipino* in promoting the Filipino language, particularly in the areas of Philippine literature and language teaching.

Sikolohiya ng Bata: The Filipino Child, Social Relevance under Martial Law and the Newly-Restored Democracy

On the night of September 20, 1972, the eve of the declaration of martial law by Ferdinand Marcos, the Diliman Campus of the University of the Philippines was tense with students chanting "Marcos, Hitler, Diktador, Tuta." It was not the first time that this familiar refrain was heard but the Diliman community that night sensed something different. Perhaps it was because the students were no longer chanting. They were actually cursing Marcos in great anger and hate. Perhaps it was the tone of voice or intensity of the shouting: "What has Marcos done this time?" one would surely ask.

As people turned on their radios late that night, announcers expressed their displeasure with Marcos. After a minute or two, these broadcasts went off the air. One might not have realized the political significance of the incident at that time. The next morning the few remaining stations that were still operational only transmitted music or other streams of senseless babble. One station broadcast a puzzling series of questions about what was going on outside the radio station. Essentially, he was asking his companions just exactly what was happening. They did not know. It was unusual to hear a radio announcer asking for news from his listeners.

People then felt a compelling need to be informed and to communicate. Fear and unrest swept across the University of the Philippines campus in Diliman. The facilities of the University radio station, DZUP, were destroyed by soldiers, putting to naught the efforts of a former professor of Speech and Drama who had personally developed the radio facilities of the University by bringing into the country every piece of equipment across the years. Later it was learned that the University Press was also rendered inoperative. Emerenciana Arcellana, a political scientist, exclaimed "This day shall go down in history as the worst day, as a day of infamy, in the Philipines."

A media blackout followed for what seemed to be a long, long time. No newspapers, no radio, no television, just word of mouth. Only a few would have witnessed encounters. Only a few would have heard a frightening exchange of gunfire. But there were all sorts of unverified reports. Never had the role of media as a source of information been so pronounced as in those turbulent times, when media was suppressed.

Media resumed operations only after the Marcos government secured control of all media outlets. The first news, broadcast in a foreign language, was the declaration of martial law. The return of state-controlled media, however, was not exactly welcomed because by then, freedom of expression was severely curtailed. Newspapers critical of the government were forcibly closed. The Marcos dictatorship issued guidelines which controlled every form of media and communication. Even word of mouth was placed under control. A person could be arrested for the embarrassing crime of "rumor-mongering."

The suspension of the writ of habeas corpus and the years of martial law adversely affected Filipinos from all walks of life. Physicists, historians, political scientists, writers, and journalists were detained for political reasons. However, it was business as usual for American-oriented psychologists, as though they were the most apolitical among the academics and the professionals. Psychology conventions were not bereft of heated discussions on social issues, but the establishment psychologists remained non-committal, if not lukewarm, to say the least, on the martial law regime.

The powers-that-be did not waste time making it known that they meant business. Slogans were interminably aired on radio and TV in the name of the "New Society." "*Sa ikauunlad ng bayan, disiplina ang kailangan*" ("For the country's progress, discipline is needed.")

As soon as the people realized the dictatorship had no sense of humor, even otherwise sensible writers had to censor their own writing before publication. Still, the spirit of dissent continued. *Focus* magazine unwittingly published a seemingly harmless poem in which the first letter of each line, when read downward together with the other first letters, formed the words "MARCOS HITLER DIKTADOR TUTA." (*Tuta*, or puppy, is the Filipino word for "puppet.") It was too late for the authorities to withdraw the magazine from the newsstands for the copies were immediately sold out.

The attempt to control communication was thorough. It became dangerous to hold on to any material the regime considered subversive. Mere possession was considered a crime. Even academicians who used to collect protest literature burnt their collections. People had to be creative in their manner of expressing dissent in order not to incur the ire of the dictatorship. Reminiscent of the *zarzuela* or the so-called subversive plays popular after the Philippine-American war at the turn of the century, the drama took the form of a chameleon play depending upon the audience.

The New Order took its toll on the ranks of young psychology students and members of the *Pambansang Samahan sa Sikolohiyang Pilipino*. Aware of the contradiction between textbook psychology and the reality outside the classroom, psychologist Carol Pagaduan asked why so much time should be spent in the psychology laboratory while Filipinos starved in Central Luzon. She was arrested and detained by the military. Landlord exploitation of the peasants drew psychologist Elizabeth Protacio-Marcelino to the ricefields of Nueva Ecija for her psychology research. She landed in Bicutan instead. Political psychologist Tina Montiel and her child suffered as well. Wives, mothers, brothers and children were separated from parents, husbands, friends and colleagues but the cruelty of martial law was harder on the poor, defenseless children.

Psychologists had to act. Elizabeth Protacio-Marcelino spearheaded the movement to help the children of political detainees and the young victims of militarization. She established the Children's Rehabilitation Center (CRC) for this purpose. Brutalized not only by the military but also by economic realities, the Filipino child, be he in food-starved Negros, the streets of Manila, or the resorts of Pagsanjan, needed all the assistance he could get, psychological or otherwise.

The child holds a special place in the psyche of the Filipino. In comparison with their counterparts in Europe and America, the Westernized/Christianized Filipinos pay more attention and veneration to the child Jesus (*Santo Niño*) than the adult Jesus (Terada 1987). Discouraged by the state of child psychology studies in the country, Ventura (1985) characterized the researches from 1968 to 1980 as "sporadic." She found "relatively well-researched areas of study" such as Piagetian cognitive development, but too many studies were "prefaced as exploratory or preliminary." Many more areas of study "have attracted only cursory attention." Most of the subjects of either sex were urban children seven to 12 years old, who participated in short, one-session testing. Almost half of the studies (43.59 percent) were on socio-emotional aspects of child psychology. Ventura recommended that researchers "look beyond testing and utilize alternative modes of study which would allow for a more meaningful investigation of child behavior." *Sikolohiyang Pilipino* methods emphasizing "naturalistic approaches" should prove useful in the "discovery of patterns of behavior which could lead to more culturally-relevant conceptualizations of Filipino child psychology." The need for counselling techniques, leisure and study programs, measures and approaches more suited to the Filipino child, not to mention norms, standards, and scientific theories, led psychologists Esther A. Reyes and Elizabeth Ventura, anthropologist Leticia Lagmay, and their colleagues to establish an indigenous child psychology-oriented organization. The *Samahang Pilipino sa Sikolohiya ng Bata* (Child Psychology Association of the Philippines) was established in July 1982 with Reyes, director of the Child Study Center, Philippine Normal College, as founding President.

The American-backed Marcos dictatorship virtually robbed the children of their future. The regime snatched away the best years from the young. Accordingly, the intensity of feeling and the degree of commitment to the *sikolohiyang Pilipino* movement is now more visible among them. The risk of being arrested for defying martial law, however, did not deter the undergraduate psychology major from going off campus and joining the people in deliberating issues such as the sham elections. It was ironic for psychologists to be calmly gathering data to test a fine theoretical point as the nation sought freedom from a greedy dictatorship. The Filipino psychologist had to do better than that. He had to act and move others to act. However, establishment psychology did not exactly welcome the idea of psychologists in fishing and farming communities instead of the laboratory or the clinic. Roberto Galvez, a junior undergraduate student of community psychology at the University of the Philippines in Diliman, confronted the establishment psychologists with questions of relevance to Philippine realities. He chided the alienated devotees of Freud, Skinner, and other Western psychologists in his poem entitled "*Sa mga Pilipinong Sikolohistang Nawawala sa Sarili* ("To the Filipino Psychologists Who Lost Their Soul and Identity"):

> *Hindi si Freud ang aking inusal*
> *nang ilantad ni Anna Marie at Isabel Lopez*
> *ang kanilang kaluluwa sa ECP* [Experimental Cinema of the
>   Philippines]
> *at nang sa makintab na papel ng* Playboy
> *ay tumanyag ang mga Pilipina*
> *dahil kay Tetchie.*

> [Freud's name I did not whisper
> as Anna Marie and Isabel Lopez bared
> everything at the ECP
> and when the Filipina got to be known
> through the glossy pages of *Playboy*
> because of Tetchie.]

> *Hindi si Skinner ang nasa dulo*
> *ng aking rosaryo nang pagpistahan*
> *ng mga daga ang halos buto nang sanggol*
> *na naiwan ng ina sa barung-barong*
> *upang umutang ng gatas*
> *sa tindahan.*

> [Skinner was not in my rosary beads
> as the rats feasted on the bone-thin child
> left behind by his mother in the makeshift house
> to borrow milk
> from the store.]

Hindi si Jung ang aking pinalanginan
nang tumaghoy ang mga ninuno
sa pagkawasak ng tribung Kalinga
at pagka-piit ng Ilog-Chico
upang patakbuhin ang mga
makina ng dambuhala.

[To Jung I did not pray
as ancestors bewailed
the rape of the Kalinga tribe
and the captivity of the Chico river
so the monster's machine can run.]

Hindi si Harris ang aking pinagkumpisalan
kung okey ako at okey rin
ang mamamayan sa panahong ang busal
na pantapal ay panglamang tiyan na
at piring sa mata ay nasa komiks,
sine at pahayagan pa.

[To Harris I did not confess
If I am O.K. and if the people are O.K.
at a time when the cob is both muzzle and food
and the eyes cannot see through the comic books,
movies and newspapers.]

Hindi si Rogers ang aking niluhuran
nang sakmalin ng teargas
at paputukin ng truncheon
ang ulo't slogan
hindi sa mga group dynamics
kundi sa daang Mendiola.

[To Rogers I did not kneel
when heads and slogans
were seized by teargas
and blasted by truncheons
not in group dynamics
but in the street of Mendiola.]

Hindi, hindi ko sila sasambahin
sa kung ano ang kalikasan ng tao
sapagkat sikolohista akong
ayaw mawala sa sarili
at sa lipunang hindi naman nila ginagalawan.

[No, I don't worship their theories
on the nature of man
for I am a psychologist
who refuses to lose his mind and identity
and awareness of his society.]

Galvez defied the establishment psychologists as he defied the Marcos government by founding *Buklod-Isip* or *Bukluran sa Sikolohiyang Pilipino* in 1981. Not content with promoting social awareness, analysis and criticism, *Buklod-Isip* advocates a socially relevant psychology. The excesses of the Marcos regime and the vigilance demanded by the democratic space afforded under the leadership of Corazon Aquino made it easy for members of *Buklod* to chart their course of action.

In search of a psychology which reflects Philippine realities and answers to the needs of Philippine society, the members of *Buklod-Isip* solemnly renewed their commitment to the *adhikain* (goals) of the organization in an annual rite of *muling-panunumpa* (renewal of commitment). Poetry and passion were shared with a sense of urgency as the dictatorship was prone to rear its ugly head at any time, be it at the *Buklod* reunion or *muling panunumpa* in the ricefields of Bulacan, or the lonely beach at Cavite, or the supposedly more commodious *Pook ni Maria Makiling* in the mountains of Laguna where historian Romeo V. Cruz shared his views on nationalism.

The charter members of *Buklod-Isip* initiated the formation of a convening group which finally established in September 1982 a federation of psychology student organizations, the *Pederasyon ng mga Mag-aaral sa Sikolohiya* or Psych Fed, after years of unsuccessful attempts at getting organized. Undergraduate psychology students from exclusive schools learned more about *sikolohiyang Pilipino* from their peers and from young instructors who were exposed to the *sikolohiyang Pilipino* literature. The initial concern with winning quiz shows to enhance school image was eventually replaced by a greater concern for social relevance and action. The students started hurling disturbing questions at teachers bound by mainstream American psychology.

By the year 1987, the movement for social change was at a crisis. Street parliamentarians chose to remain silent and passive to "give Cory a chance." Unlike that of Marcos' reign, the new dispensation had promise of being democratic, just and

Pagmamalasakit (concern), *pagtulong* and *pagdamay* (helping), and *pakikibaka* (exerting pressure) have been identified as examples of the more enduring *paninindigan* (commitment or conviction).

The EDSA revolution was premised on *katarungan, kalayaan, karangalan: Rebulusyon sa bisikleta*

> patriotic. "People power," the crucial variable in the over-
> throw of the Marcos government, fizzled out as members of
> people's organizations chose to be less active and critical in the
> construction of the "new" state. The "revolutionaries" of
> EDSA surrendered democracy to the new electorate...Was the
> revolution over? Has the EDSA revolution achieved genuine
> peace, justice and democracy for the people? (Carunungan
> 1989)

As the euphoria brought about by People's Power in the so-called EDSA revolution slowly dissipated, it finally became clear that the struggle had to go on. Armed conflict raged from the countryside to the cities, sowing uncertainty and fear among the people. Unemployment rates skyrocketed while the economy plummeted due to the burden of a gargantuan foreign debt, inherited from the Marcos regime. Nationalist mass leaders, cultural workers and even clergymen were harassed, abducted or killed. Human rights violations by an unstable and uncontrollable military reached heights comparable only to the record of the Marcos regime. Kordon, et al. (1988), in their study on the psychological effects of political repression in Argentina, found out that through repression, the missing are presumed to be dead, the dead are relegated to oblivion, dissidence attains the status of a mental disease and the living are brutalized into silence and guilt. The result of the study in Argentina finds continuing relevance in the Philippines in the light of parallel cases of political repression, "involuntary disappearance" and "salvaging" (summary execution). The play *Desaparecidos* is still as relevant under the Aquino regime as when it was staged during the time of the hated Marcos dictatorship.

The Aquino apologists and defenders of her "total war" policy were not above closing radio stations and other forms of media in the interest of national security. The guardians of morals would not even risk showing *Ora Pro Nobis*, an internationally acclaimed Filipino movie on human rights, in Philippine commercial theaters.

Marcos' stroke of genius in abolishing Congress and turning its halls into a museum became a matter of history as the landed elite and the politics of the '50s once again lorded it over Philippine society. The congressional and senatorial elections of 1987 erased all hopes of change coming from the old politicians as the Aquino administration supported a bureaucracy bent only on maintaining the status quo. Instead, change now manifests itself in the emergence of a new awareness of being Filipino. The Filipino now uses the indigenous Filipino language not only in Manila and Davao but also in Yokohama, Hongkong, Munich, Riyadh, Rome, San Francisco and New York. A new level of national awareness is felt even in popular culture. Once again, peasant, labor and student protests are mounting, hurling *sikolohiyang Pilipino*--body and soul--into the continuing struggle for justice and liberation.

REFERENCES

I. Works of History and Commentary

Agoncillo, Teodoro
1974

Filipino Nationalism 1872-1970. Quezon City: R.P. Garcia Publishing Co.

Alfonso, Amelia B.
1977

"Towards developing Philippine psychology: language-related issues in teaching and research." Paper prepared for the Fourth Conference of the Asian Association of National Languages, University of Malaysia, Kuala Lumpur, Malaysia, April 25-30, 1977.

Atal, Yogesh
1979

"The Call for Indigenization." *The Indigenization of Social Science in Asia.* Jan J. Loubser, ed. The International Federation of Social Science Organizations. Occasional Paper No. 1 Canada: Mutual Press Ltd., Ottawa, 1-21.

Bartolome, Jose Ma.
1985

"The pitfalls of Filipino personality." *Sikolohiyang Pilipino: Isyu, Pananaw at Kaalaman (New Directions in Indigenous Psychology).* Allen Agannon & S. Ma. Assumpta David, RVM, eds. Manila: National Book Store, Inc., 531-37.

Bauzon, Leslie E.
1985

Foreword to Evelyn Tan Cullamar's *Babaylanism in Negros: 1896-1907.* Quezon City: New Day Publishers, 1986, vii-x.

Bennagen, Ponciano L.   "Social science development in the Philippines."
1985   *Asian Perspectives in Social Science*. The Institute
                               of Social Sciences International Studies Series No.
                               7. W.R. Geddes, ed. Seoul, Korea: Seoul National
                               University Press, 91-98.

Boring, Edward G.   *A History of Experimental Psychology*. New York:
1929   Appleton-Century Crofts, 699 pp.

Casiño, Eric S.   "Politics, religion, and social stratification: The
1973   case of Cagayan Sulu." *The Muslim Filipinos: A
                               Book of Readings*. Nagasura T. Madale, ed. Quezon
                               City: Alemar Phoenix Publishing House, Inc., 1981.

Castillo, Gelia T.   "A view from Southeast Asia." SEADAG, *Ameri-
1968   can Research on Southeast Asia Development.
                               Asian and American Views*. New York: The Asia
                               Society, 20-49.

Chirino, Pedro   *Relacion de las Islas Filipinas*. Rome: 1604; 2nd
1604   Ed. Manila: Imprenta de Esteban Balbas, 1890.
                               Cited by Teodoro A. Agoncillo in his introduction
                               to the book *Introduction to Modern Pilipino Lit-
                               erature*. Epifanio San Juan, Jr., ed., New York:
                               Twayne Publishers, Inc., 1974, 3, 228.

Comision Nacional   "Poesias por Jose Rizal." *Escritos de Jose Rizal*
de Historia,   (Tomo III: Obras Literarias. Libro Primero). Ma-
Republica de Filipinas   nila: Comision Nacional de Historia, 171 pp.
1972

Constantino, Renato   *Dissent and Counter-Consciousness*. Quezon City,
1970   Philippines: Malaya Books, Inc.

1975a   *A History of the Philippines: From the Spanish
                               Colonization to the Second World War*. New York:
                               Monthly Review Press.

1975b   *The Philippines: A Past Revisited*. Manila, Philip-
                               pines: Renato Constantino.

Cullamar, Evelyn Tan
1986

Babaylanism in Negros: 1896-1907. Quezon City: New Day Publishers.

David, Randolf
1977

"Ang pagkagapos ng agham panlipunang Pilipino" [The colonization of Philippine social science"]. *Ulat ng Ikalawang Pambansang Kumperensya sa Sikolohiyang Pilipino* [Proceedings of the Second National Conference on Filipino Psychology]. Diliman, Lunsod Quezon: Pambansang Samahan sa Sikolohiyang Pilipino.

del Castillo, Teofilo y
Tuazon and Buenaventura
S. Medina, Jr.
1972

Philippine Literature: From Ancient Times to the Present. Quezon City, Philippines, 546 pp.

Enriquez, Virgilio G.
1974

"Mga batayan ng Sikolohiyang Pilipino sa kultura at kasaysayan" ["The Bases of Filipino Psychology in Culture and History"]. *Sikolohiyang Pilipino: Batayan sa Kasaysayan, Perspektibo, Mga Konsepto at Bibliograpiya.* Diliman, Lunsod Quezon: Unibersidad ng Pilipinas. *1,* 1-29. Also included in *General Education Journal. 29* (First semester, 1975-1976), 61-88.

1975

"Developing concepts and approaches in Philippine psychology." [Unpublished research report to the National Research Council of the Philippines].

1977

"Filipino psychology in the Third World." *Philippine Journal of Psychology 10* (1), 3-18.

1988

From Colonial to Liberation Psychology: The Indigenous Perspective in Philippine Psychology. Teaching and Research Exchange Fellowships Report No. 3. Southeast Asian Studies Program. Singapore: Institute of Southeast Asian Studies.

Galvez, Bobby
[Roberto]
1985

"Sa mga Pilipinong sikolohistang nawawala sa sarili" ["To Filipino psychologists without consciousness and identity."] *Mithi 11* (12), 112-13.

Gonzales, Andrew B.
1982

"Filipinization of the social sciences: a red herring?" *Social Sciences Information 10* (2), 9-13. Also included in *New Directions in Indigenous Psychology. Sikolohiyang Pilipino: Isyu, Pananaw at Kaalaman*. Allen Aganon and S. Ma. Assumpta David, eds. Metro Manila: National Book Store, 91-104.

Graumann, Carl E.
1972

"The state of psychology" (part one), *International Journal of Psychology 7* (2), 123-34.

Grimm, William J.
1988

"Internationalization of Japan impossible," *Asahi Evening News*, August 4, 1988.

Harris, M.
1976

"History and significance of the emic/etic distinction." *Annual Review of Anthropology 5, 329-50.*

Hayter, T.
1971

Aid as Imperialism. Middlesex, England: Penguin.

Hoshino, Akira and
Takao Umemoto
1986

"Japanese psychology: historical review and recent trends." *Psychology Moving East: The Status of Western Psychology in Asia and Oceania.* Geoffrey Blowers and Allison Tuttle, eds. Boulder, Colorado: Westview Press, 183-96

Jacob, Betty M.
and Philip E. Jacob
1977

"The diplomacy of cross-national collaborative research." *Bonds Without Bondage.* Krishna Kumar, ed. Honolulu: East-West Center, 1979, 85-101.

Jahoda, Gustav
1976a

"In pursuit of the emic-etic distinction: Can we ever capture it?" Symposium on the Importance of Theory in Cross-Cultural Psychology, Third International Congress, International Association for Cross-Cultural Psychology, Tilburg, University of Holland, July 12-16, 1976.

1976b

"Mediating between extremes: An approach to transitional social science plows." Honolulu, Hawaii: East-West Center (March 30).

Kleden, Ignas
1987

"Southeast Asia: cultural adaptation or cultural doubt?" *New Asian Visions 4* (2), 4-29.

Lagmay, Alfredo V.
1984

"Western psychology in the Philippines: Impact and response." *International Journal of Psychology 19*, 31-44.

Lagmay, Leticia A.
1978

"Philippine culture-personality research: a review." *Agham-Tao 1*, 111-24. Included in *Sikolohiyang Pilipino: Teorya, Metodo at Gamit (Filipino Psychology: Theory, Method & Application)*. Rogelia PePua, ed. Lunsod Quezon: Surian ng Sikolohiyang Pilipino, 1982, 240-50.

Lawless, Robert
1969

"An evaluation of Philippine Culture-Personality research." Monograph Series No. 3 Asian Center, University of the Philippines. Quezon City, Philippines: University of the Philippines Press, 57 pp.

Layug, Ma. Estela M.,
Joanne Q.S. Ramilo-
Cantiller, and Ma. Elisa
F. Esguerra, eds.
1987

"Ang Sikolohiya sa Silangan: Pinagmulan at Patutunguhan" ["Psychology in the East: Source and Direction"]. Unpublished compilation. University of the Philippines, Diliman, Quezon City.

Licuanan, Patricia B.
1985

Psychology in the Philippines: history and current trends. *Philippine Studies 33*, 67-86.

Meichenbaum, Donald
1988

"What happens when the "brute data" of psychological inquiry are meanings: nurturing a dialogue between hermeneutics and empiricism." *Hermeneutics and Psychological Theory (Interpretive Perspectives on Personality, Psychotherapy, and Psychopathology)*. S.B. Messer, L.A. Sass [and] R.L. Woolfolk, eds. New Brunswick and London: Rutgers University Press, 116-30.

Moghaddam, Fathali M.
1987

"Psychology in the three worlds: as reflected by the crisis in social psychology and the move toward indigenous Third-World psychology." *American Psychologist 42* (10), 912-20.

Murphy, Gardner and   *Asian Psychology*. New York: Basic Books, Inc.,
L.B. Murphy [eds.]   238 pp.
1972

Navarro, Jovina, ed.   "The plight of the newly-arrived immigrants."
1974   *Diwang Pilipino* [Pilipino Consciousness]. Davis,
                                      California: Asian American Studies, Department
                                      of Applied Behavioral Sciences, University of Cali-
                                      fornia, 17-44.

Ocampo, Nilo S.   *Katutubo, Muslim, Kristyano: Palawan, 1621-
1985   1901*. Kolonya, Alemanya: Publikasyon Blg. I ng
                                      Bahay-Saliksikan ng Kasaysayan (BAKAS).

O'Connell, D. C.   "The changing faces of European psychology:
1970   Germany." Paper presented at the meeting of the
                                      American Psychological Association, Miami Beach,
                                      September 1970.

Panganiban, Jose Villa   *Diksyunaryo-Tesaoro: Pilipino-Ingles*. Lungsod
1972   Quezon, Pilipinas: Manlapaz Publishing Co.

Panganiban, Jose Villa and   *Panitikan ng Pilipinas* [Philippine Literature].
Consuelo Torres Panganiban   Lunsod ng Quezon: Bede's Publishing House,
1954   248 pp.

Panlasigui, Isidoro   *The Language Problems of the Philippines*. Quezon
1962   City. 97 pp.

Pe, Rogelia E.   "*Ang paggamit ng Filipino sa pagtuturo ng
1980   sikolohiya: 1965-1980*" ["The Filipino language
                                      as medium in the teaching of psychology: 1965-
                                      1980"]. *Philippine Social Sciences and Humani-
                                      ties Review XLIV* (1-4), 213-42.

Phillips, Derek L.   *Abandoning Method*. San Francisco, California:
1973   Josey-Bass, Inc.

Quirino, Carlos   *Filipinos at War*. Philippines: Vera-Reyes, Inc.
1981

Rood, Steven
1985

"Language and Philippine Social Science." Paper read at the First National Philippine Studies Conference, Quezon City, February 11-13, 1985. Included in *Sikolohiyang Pilipino: Isyu, Pananaw at Kaalaman (New Directions in Indigenous Psychology)*. Allen Aganon and S. Ma. Assumpta David, RVM, eds. Quezon City: National Book Store, 76-90.

Salazar, Zeus A.
1983a

The Ethnic Dimension: Papers on Philippine Culture, History and Psychology. Ang Tambuli. Special Issue No. 1 Counselling Center for Filipinos, Caritas Association for the City of Cologne.

1983b

"Four Filiations in Philippine Psychological Thought." *Sikolohiyang Pilipino: Isyu, Pananaw at Kaalaman (New Directions in Indigenous Psychology)*. Allen Agannon and Ma. Assumpta David, eds. Manila: National Book Store, 1985, 194-214.

Samonte, Elena
1979

"The Status of Psychology at the De La Salle University." Unpublished manuscript. Diliman, Quezon City: University of the Philippines.

Samson, Laura
1980

"The politics of understanding Philippine culture." *Diliman Review 22* (4), 45-48. Also included in *Sikolohiyang Pilipino: Isyu, Pananaw at Kaalaman (New Directions in Indigenous Psychology)*. Allen Aganon and Ma. Assumpta David, eds. Metro Manila, Philippines: National Book Store, 538-45.

San Buenaventura,
Mario
1985

"Ang kaganapan ng sikolohiyang Pilipino: pagsasakatutubo, pagka-agham at pagka-Pilipino" ["The vision of sikolohiyang Pilipino: indigenization, science and national culture"]. *Sikolohiyang Pilipino: Isyu, Pananaw at Kaalaman (New Directions in Indigenous Psychology)*. Allen Aganon and Ma. Assumpta David, eds. Metro Manila, Philippines: National Book Store, 228-54.

Santiago, Carmen E.
[and] Virgilio G.
Enriquez
1976

"Tungo sa makapilipinong pananaliksik" ["Towards a Filipino-oriented research"]. *Sikolohiyang Pilipino: Mga Ulat at Balita 1* (4), 3-10, 19. Also included in *Sikolohiyang Pilipino: Teorya, Metodo at Gamit (Filipino Psychology: Theory, Method and Application)*. Rogelia Pe-Pua, ed. Lunsod Quezon: Surian ng Sikolohiyang Pilipino, 1982 155-60.

Sarra, Eleanor
1973

"Ang sikolohiya sa Pilipinas at si Agustin S. Alonzo, sikolohista." ["Philippine psychology and Agustin S. Alonzo, psychologist"]. Paper read at the *Panayam sa Sikolohiya IV, Palma Hall, College of Arts and Sciences, University of the Philippines, Diliman, Quezon City.*

Sechrest, Lee and
George Guthrie
1974

"Psychology of, by, and for Filipinos." *Philippine Studies: Geography, Archaeology, Psychology and Literature*. Special Report No. 10.

Sicat, Gerardo
1976

"A living Filipino language: A challenge to social scientists." *Seminar-Workshop on Enhancing the Role of Social Scientists in National Development. Bulletin No. 66*. Taguig, Metro Manila: National Research Council of the Philippines.

Tennant, Edward A.
1987

A book review of *Philippine World-View. International Journal of Intercultural Relations 11* (4), 414-17.

Veneracion, Jaime B.
1986

Kasaysayan ng Bulakan. Kolonya, Alemanya: Bahay Saliksikan ng Kasaysayan, 241 pp.

Ventura, Elizabeth
1980

"Filipino psychology: some recent trends and developments." Unpublished manuscript. University of the Philippines, Diliman, Quezon City.

Villacorta, Wilfrido
1980

"Western influences on social science teaching in Philippine Universities." *Sikolohiyang Pilipino: Isyu, Pananaw at Kaalaman*. Allen Agannon & Ma. Assumpta David, eds. Metro Manila, Philippines: National Bookstore, 1985, 49-66.

Wakefield, Jerome
1988

"Hermeneutics and Empiricism: A Commentary on Donald Miechenbaum." *Hermeneutics and Psychological Theory: Intepretative Perspective on Personality, Psychotherapy and Psychopathology.* Stanley B. Messer, Louis A. Sass and Robert L. Woolfolk, eds. New Brunswick and London: Rutgers University Press.

Watson, Robert I.
1963

The Great Psychologists: from Aristotle to Freud. Philadelphia: J. P. Lippincott Co.

1968

"Recent developments in the historiography of American psychology." *Isis 59* (197, part 2), 199-205.

Wenceslao, Ma. Theresa and Lia Pison
1986

"On Philippine psychology: an interview with Virgilio G. Enriquez." *Kaya Tao 8* (1), 131-46, Journal of the Behavioral Sciences Department, De La Salle University.

II. Psychological/Social Science Research Studies

Abasolo-Domingo, Fe
1961

"Child-rearing practices in barrio Cruz na Ligas." *Philippine Journal of Psychology 8*, 1978.

Acuña, Jasmin
1987

The Development of Thinking Among Filipinos: Implications for Public Education. Manila: Publications Office of the De La Salle University Research Center, 67 pp.

Adea, Marivere
1974

"*Mga kaugaliang Pilipino sa pag-aaruga ng bata.*" *Tao at Lipunan.* Virgilio G. Enriquez, Pemari Banzuela at Ma. Carmen Galan, eds. Diliman, Quezon City: University of the Philippines, 296 pp.

Agannon, Allen and Ma. Assumpta David, eds.
1985

Sikolohiyang Pilipino: Isyu, Pananaw at Kaalaman (New Directions in Indigenous Psychology). Manila: National Book Store, Inc., 567 pp.

Aldaba-Lim, Estefania
1966

"The role of parents in the character formation of the child." *The Filipino Family: Selected Readings*. Lunsod Quezon: Alemar-Phoenix Publishing House, 38-43.

Alejo, Albert E.
1986

"*Hermeneutika ng loob: isang landas ng pagunawa sa pakikisangkot.*" ["Hermeneutics of *loob*: a path to understanding 'involvement'"]. Unpublished M.A. (Philosophy) thesis. Loyola Heights, Quezon City: Ateneo de Manila University.

Alfonso, Amelia
1974

"*Malayang paggunita: ang epekto ng agwat, paguulit, at pagsasalin*" ["Free recall: The effect of spacing, repetition and translation"]. *Diwa: Dyornal sa Sikolohiya, Agham, Kultura at Lipunang Pilipino 3* (1-2).

Almario, Gundelina
1972

"*Ang pagmumura bilang sanhi ng pagkagalit at paghihiganti. Sikolohiya ng Wika: Working Papers in Psycholinguistics*. Virgilio G. Enriquez at Lilia Antonio, eds. Diliman, Quezon City: University of the Philippines.

Almendral, S.A.
1969

"A conceptual framework for child-rearing in the Philippines." Centro Escolar University Graduate and Faculty Studies, 20 pp.

Alonto, Norhata M.
1975

"*Ang batang Pilipino mula lampin hanggang pantalon.*" Unpublished paper. Quezon City: Department of Psychology, University of the Philippines.

Avila, Madelene, Ma.
Angeli Diaz and
Cristina Rodriguez
1987

"Konsepto ng Katarungan." *Kaya Tao 9* (1), 47-54. Journal of the Behavioral Sciences Department, De La Salle University.

Azurin, Arnold M.
1993

Reinventing the Filipino: Sense of Being and Becoming. Diliman, Q.C.: CSSP Publishing and UP Press.

Bailen, Jerome
1967

"A Palawan babaylan's views of disease causation." *The U.P. Anthropology Bulletin 3* (1), 6-9.

Bilmes, Jack
1973

"Misinformation and ambiguity in verbal interaction: A Northern Thai example."

Bonifacio, Armando
1976

"*Hinggil sa kaisipang Pilipino*" ["On Filipino thought"]. *Ulat ng Unang Pambansang Kumperensya sa Sikolohiyang Pilipino* [Proceedings of the First National Conference on Filipino Psychology]. L.F. Antonio, E.S. Reyes, R.E. Pe and N.R. Almonte, eds., Lunsod Quezon: Pambansang Samahan sa Sikolohiyang Pilipino, 24-48.

Bonifacio, Manuel F.
1980

Presidential Address. *Kamalayang Etniko at Pambansang Pananagutan*. [Ethnic Consciousness and National Responsibility]. *Ika-anim na Pambansang Kumperensya sa Sikolohiyang Pilipino*. Bicol State University, October 23, 1980.

Bostrom, Lynn C.
1968

"Filipino *Bahala na* and American Fatalism." *Silliman University Journal 51*, 399-413.

Brislin, Richard W.
1976

"Comparative research methodology: Cross-cultural studies." *International Journal of Psychology 11*, 215-49.

1977

"Ethical issues influencing the acceptance and rejection of cross-cultural researchers who visit various countries." *Issues in Cross-Cultural Research (Annals of the New York Academy of sciences) 285*. Lenore Leob Adler, ed., 185-202.

———
and Fahy Holwill
1976

"Indigenous views of the writing of behavioral social scientists: Towards increased cross-cultural understanding." *International Journal of Intercultural Relations*.

Bulatao, Jaime
1979a

"Oh, That Terrible Task of Teachers to Teach Psychology in the Philippines." *Philippine Journal of Psychology 1*, 33-37.

1979b   "Relevance in Philippine Psychology." *Essays and Studies of Father Jaime C. Bulatao.* Rosalinda Sanchez-Castiglioni, comp. (Quezon City: Ateneo de Manila University), 251-57.

Cabezon, Dionisio   "Introduction to Psychology" (Section 4). *The Unitas Reader 50,* 182-86.
1977

Calderon, Sofronio G.   *Talasalitaan ng Inang Wika.* Manila: Inang Wika Publication Co.
1957

Campbell, Donald T.   "Convergent and discriminant validation by the multitrait-multimethod matrix." *Psychology Bulletin 56,* 81-105.
and D.W. Fiske
1964

Carreon, Manuel   *Philippine Studies in Mental Measurement.* New York: World Book, 175 pp.
1923

Carlota, Annadaisy   "The development of the *Panukat ng Pagkataong Pilipino* (PPP)." *Philippine Journal of Educational Measurement 4* (1), 55-68.
1985

Carunungan, Maria   "To build a people's culture: The Visayan experience." *Makiisa 1* (4).
1989

Chan-Yap, Gloria   "Chinese influences in the Tagalog language." Unpublished Ph.D. (Linguistics) dissertation. Ateneo de Manila University, Quezon City.
1973

Church, A. Timothy   Personality research in a non-western culture: The Philippines. *Psychological Bulletin 102* (2), 272-92.
1987

Cipres-Ortega, Susan   *"Sikolohiyang Pilipino: Mga Implikasyon sa Pagtuturo at Pag-aaral"* ["Filipino Psychology: Implications for Teaching and Learning"]. Paper read at the Annual meeting of the Linguistic Society of the Philippines, Philippine Normal College, May 6, 1980.
1980

Concha, Jesus A.   *Philippine National Formulary.* National Science Development Board. Metro Manila: Bicutan, Tagig.
1980

Crisanto, Ma. Trinidad,
Milagros Herrera,
Flordeliza Logbao
and Grace Orteza
1985

*Sikopatolohiyang Pilipino: Kasaysayan, Katu-
tubong Konsepto, at Pamamaraan.* Taft.

de Guzman, Maria
Odulio
1968

*Bagong Diksyonaryo Pilipino-Ingles/Ingles-
Pilipino.* Manila: National Bookstore.

de Leon, Felipe M., Jr.
1981

"Towards a people's art." *Lipunan.* Series II. Vol.
III, 1-15.

de Mesa, Jose M.
1987

"With a Listening Heart." *Solidarity with the
Culture: Studies in Theological Re-rooting.*
Maryhill School of Theology, Quezon City.

de Padua, Ludivina S.,
Gregorio C. Lugod,
[and] Juan V. Pancho
1977

Handbook on Philippine Medicinal Plants. Vol-
ume 1 *Technical Bulletin 2* (3).

de Peralta, Patricia A.
1984

*"Pagpapahalagang hatid ng mga popular na 'sarita
idi ugma' mula Ilocos Norte"* [Values in Ilocos Norte
folk stories"]. Unpublished M.A. (Psychology) thesis. Department of Psychology, University of the
Philippines, Diliman, Quezon City.

_____and
Angeles D. Racelis
1974

"Mga uri ng pahiwatig". ["Classification of
cues"]. *Sikolinggwistikang Pilipino.* Virgilio G.
Enriquez, ed. Diliman, Quezon City: University of
the Philippines Press, 1-22.

de Vera, Ma. Gracia,
Agnes Montano and
Edgardo A. Angeles
1975

"Ang metodo ng pagtatanung-tanong" ["The
method of *pagtatanung-tanong"*]. Report prepared
for Psychology 180 (Social Psychology). College
of Arts and Sciences, University of the Philippines,
November 11, 1975.

Diaz-Guerrero, Rogelio
1977

"A Mexican Psychology." *American Psychologist 32* (11) 934-44.

Diokno, Jose W.   "A Filipino concept of Justice." *Batas at*
1981   *Katarungan*. Vol. I, No. 1, February, 1-17. Also
                         included in Allen Aganon and Ma. Assumpta David,
                         RVM (eds.); *Sikolohiyang Pilipino, Isyu, Pananaw*
                         at Kaalaman, pp. 271-87. Manila: National Book-
                         store, 1985.

Elequin, Eleanor   "Educational Goals, Aims and Objectives." Re-
1974   port of a study by a working group in Asia. Unesco-
                         Nier Regional Programme for Education Research
                         in Asia. Tokyo, Japan: National Institute for
                         Educational Research, 114.

1978   *"Isang sulyap ng isang mananaliksik sa musikang*
                         Pilipino at ang kahalagahan nito sa kaisipang
                         Pilipino" ["A researcher's look at Pilipino music
                         and its importance to Pilipino thought"]. *Ang*
                         Pandaigdigang Pananaw ng Pilipino [The Pilipino
                         Worldview]. Diliman, Quezon City: Philippine
                         Psychology Research House.

1977   *Organizing for Cross-Cultural Research: Tactics*
                         in Culture Learning, Vol. V, East West Center,
                         Honolulu, Hawaii.

Enriquez, Virgilio G.   *"Talambuhay ng isang baliw: Katotohanang*
1971   *naglaho at nagbalik."* (Narrated to Marguerite
                         Sechehaye in French. Translated to Filipino from
                         the English version of Grace Rubin-Rabson).
                         Diliman Review 22 (3), 1974, 191-273.

1976a   *Sikolinggwistikang Pilipino (Wika at Lipunan,*
                         Kaasalang Pangwika, Bilinggwalismo at Suliranin
                         sa Pagpapahayag) [Filipino Psycholinguistics: Lan-
                         guage and Culture, Verbal Behavior, Bilingualism
                         and Communicative Disorders]. Diliman, Quezon
                         City: University of the Philippines Press.

1976b   *"Sikolohiyang Pilipino: perspektibo at direksyon"*
                         ["Filipino psychology: perspective and direction"].
                         Ulat ng Unang Pambansang Kumperensya sa

Sikolohiyang Pilipino [Proceedings of the First National Conference on Filipino Psychology]. Lilia F. Antonio, Esther S. Reyes, Rogelia E. Pe & Nilda R. Almonte, eds. Quezon City: Pambansang Samahan sa Sikolohiyang Pilipino, 221-43.

1977   *"Pakikisama o Pakikibaka*: Understanding the Psychology of the Filipino." Paper read at the Conference on Philippine Culture, Bay Area Bilingual Education League, Berkeley, California, April 29-30, 1977.

1978   *"Kapwa*: a core concept in Filipino social psychology." *Philippine Social Sciences and Humanities Review (Rebyu ng Agham at Humanidades ng Pilipinas)*. Vol. XLII (1-4). Also included in *Sikolohiyang Pilipino: Isyu, Pananaw at Kaalaman (New Directions in Indigenous Psychology)*. Allen Agannon & S. Ma. Assumpta David, RVM, eds. Metro Manila: National Book Store, Inc., 1985, 259-70.

1979   *"Pagkataong Pilipino: kahulugan at pananaliksik"* ["Filipino personality/personhood: significance and research"] *Sangguni 2* (1), 1979, 112-21. Also published in *Pulong 3* (1), July, 1979 and in *Filipino Thought on Man and Society*. Leonardo N. Mercado, ed. Tacloban City: Divine Word University Publications, 1980. 10-17.

1981   *"Nanganganib nga ba ang sikolohiyang Pilipino dahil sa wikang Ingles?"* *Ulat ng Ikalabindalawang seminar sa Sikolohiya ng Wika*. Susan Cipres-Ortega and the Psychology 145 (B and D) students, eds.

& Lilia F. Antonio   *Diwa: Katipunan ng Lathalaing Pangsikolohiya*. 1973   Diliman: Unibersidad ng Pilipinas, Enero, 1973.

_____and
Ma. Angeles C. Guanzon
1983

Manwal ng Panukat ng Ugali at Pagkatao [Test Manual: *Panukat ng Ugali at Pagkatao*]. Quezon City, Philippines: Philippine Psychology Research and Training House, 16 pp.

1985

"Towards the assessment of personality and culture: the *'Panukat ng Ugali at Pagkatao'.*" *Philippine Journal of Educational Measurement 4* (1), 15-54.

_____and
Elizabeth P. Marcelino
1984

Neo-colonial politics and language struggle in the Philippines (National consciousness and language in Philippines psychology: 1971-1983). Diliman, Quezon City: Akademya ng Sikolohiyang Pilipino.

1987a

"Filipino values: towards a new interpretation (Using local language as resource)." *Tagsibol 1* (1), 8-13.

1987b

"The concept of social justice in the Philippine value system." *Kaya Tao 9* (1), 1-30. Journal of the Behavioral Sciences Department, De La Salle University.

Enriquez, Jacobo P.,
[et al.]
1979

English-Tagalog-Visayan (Cebuano-Ilongo) Vocabulary: Manila: Philippine Book Co.

Estrada, Rita D.
1981

"An inquiry into sexism in the Tagalog language." *Philippine Social Sciences and Humanities Review XLV* (1-4), 427-65.

1987

"The development of psychological thought in the Philippines." Unpublished and unfinished draft on minidisc. Diliman, Quezon City: Department of Psychology, University of the Philippines, October 11, 1987.

Eugenio, Damiana
1967[6?]

"Philippine proverb lore." *Philippine Social Science Review 31* (3&4). Diliman, Quezon City: University of the Philippines, pp. 231-421.

Feliciano, Gloria D.
1965

"The limits of western social research methods in rural Philippines: The need for innovation." *Lipunan I* (1), 114-28

Fernandez, Doreen G.
1986

"Food and the Filipino." *Philippine World-View*. Virgilio G. Enriquez ed. Singapore: Southeast Asian Studies Program, Institute of Southeast Asian Studies, 20-44.

Forman, Michael L.
1973

"Philippine languages in contact: Honolulu radio station K.I.S.A." *Working Papers in Linguistics 5* (10) 137-51. Department of Linguistics. University of Hawaii.

Fox, Robert
1956

"Social class." *Area Handbook on the Philippines*. Fred Eggan, et al., eds., Vol. I. New Haven: Human Relations Area Files.

Gonzalez, Andrew,
FSC and Ma. Lourdes
S. Bautista, eds.
1981

Aspects of Language Planning and Development in the Philippines. Manila: Linguistic Society of the Philippines, 211-14.

Guillermo, Alice G.
1986

"The Filipino world-view in the visual arts. *"Philippine World View*. Virgilio G. Enriquez ed. Singapore: Southeast Asian Studies Program, Institute of Southeast Asian Studies, 45-80.

Goertz, Joseph
1965

Introduction to Theoretical Psychology (After J. Lindworsky). Cebu City: University of San Carlos. 149 pp.

Gonzalez, Lydia F.
1980

"*Ang pagtatanung-tanong: Dahilan at katangian.*" *Sikolohiyang Pilipino: Teorya, Metodo at Gamit [Filipino Psychology: Theory, Method and Application]*. Rogelia Pe-Pua, ed. Lunsod Quezon: Philippine Psychology Research and Training House, 1982, 175-86.

Guanzon, Ma. Angeles
1983

*"Ang Paggamit ng 'Panukat ng Ugali at Pagkatao'
sa Pagsasalarawan ng Kulturang Pilipino"* ["The
Use of the *Panukat ng Ugali at Pagkatao* in the
Assessment of Personality and Culture"]. Unpub-
lished Master's thesis (Psychology). Diliman,
Quezon City: University of the Philippines.

1985a

*"Ang pagsukat na sikolohikal sa pag-aaral ng
sikolohiya ng mga Pilipino."Kaya-Tao VII* (1), 1-7.

1985b

*"Paggamit ng panukat-sikolohikal sa Pilipinas:
kalagayan at mga isyu."* Sikolohiyang Pilipino:
Isyu, Pananaw at Kaalaman. (New Directions in
Indigenous Psychology)*. Allen Agannon & S. Ma.
Assumpta David, RVM, eds. Manila: National
Book Store, Inc., 341-70.

1985c

"Tungo sa pagsukat ng pagkataong Pilipino."
Malay IV (1-2), 27-39.

Guthrie, George
1972

"The shuttle box of subsistence attitudes." *Attitudes Conflict and Social Change*. New York:
Academic Press, 191-210.

Gutierrez-Gonzales,
Elizabeth
1968

"Duration of marriage and perceptual behavior of
spouses." *Philippine Journal of Psychology 1 (1),
53-61. Translated to Filipino by Belen C. Garcia.
"Ang tagal ng pagsasama ng mag-asawa at ang
kanilang persepsyon sa sarili at sa isa't isa."
Pananaliksik sa Sikolohiya*. Virgilio G. Enriquez
at Lilia Antonio, eds. Quezon City: University of
the Philippines Press, 1972, pp. 213-29.

Higginbotham,
Howard N.
1984

*Third World Challenge to Psychiatry (Culture
Accommodation and Mental Health Care)*. U.S.A.:
Institute of Culture and Communication, East-
West Center, 100-58.

Hunt, Chester L.,
Lourdes R. Quisumbing,
Socorro C. Espiritu,
Michael A. Costelo, and
Luis Q. Lacar
1987

Sociology in the Philippine Setting: A Modular Approach. Quezon City: Phoenix Publishing House.

Jocano, Felipe Landa
1975

"Ang mga babaylan at katalonan sa kinagisnang sikolohiya" ["The *babaylan* and the *katalonan* in early Philippine psychology"]. Paper read at the First National Conference in Filipino Psychology. University of the Philippines, Diliman, Quezon City, November 10, 1975.

Kakar, Sudhir
1982

Shamans, Mystics and Doctors: A Psychological Inquiry Into India and Its Healing Traditions. Boston, Massachusetts: Beacon Press Books.

Kaut, Charles, R.
1961

"Utang-na-loob: A system of contractual obligation among Tagalogs." *Southwestern Journal of Anthropology 17*, 256-72.

Kleinman, Arthur
1980

Patients and Healers in the Context of Culture: An Exploration of the Borderland between Anthropology, Medicine and Psychiatry. Berkeley and Los Angeles: University of California Press.

Kordon, Diana R.,
Lucita I. Edelman.
D.M. Lagos, E. Nicoletti,
and R.C. Bozzolo
1988

Psychological Effects of Political Repression. Buenos Aires, R. Argentina: Sudamericonal Planeta Publishing Company.

Lagmay, Alfredo V.,
Lagmay Leticia
1974

"Urbanization and change: a case study in early socialization." Diliman, Quezon City: University of the Philippines Press.

Lagmay, Alfredo V.
1976

"Bahala Na." Ulat ng Ikalawang Pambansang Kumperensiya sa Sikolohiyang Pilipino. Lunsod Quezon: Pambansang Samahan sa Sikolohiyang Pilipino, 120-30.

Lazo, Lucita S.,
Ma. Leonora
Vasquez-de Jesus and
R. Edralin-Tiglao
1976

"A survey of psychological measurement in the Philippines: industrial, clinical, and educational settings." Unpublished paper. Quezon City: Department of Psychology, University of the Philippines.

Leach, Edmund
1964

"Anthropological aspects of language: Animal categories and verbal abuse." *New Directions in the Study of Language*. Eric H. Lenneberg, ed. Cambridge, Massachusetts: The M.I.T. Press.

Lee, Emeteria P.
1973

"Measuring non-verbal academic aptitude at the University of the Philippines." Unpublished Ph.D. (Education) dissertation, University of the Philippines.

Licuanan, Patricia B.
1979

"A psychologist looks at development." *Proceedings of the Psychological Association of the Philippines 16th Annual Convention*. Alma de la Cruz, ed. Quezon City: Psychological Association of the Philippines, 54-59.

_____.
et al.
1988

"A moral recovery program: building a people--building a nation." Submitted to Senator Leticia Ramos-Shahani, April 27, 1988, 68 pp.

Lucian, Justin
1973

School Counselling: Philippine Cases and Techniques. Manila: United Publishing Co., Inc., 363 pp.

Lynch, Frank
1961

"Social acceptance." *Four Readings on Philippine Values*. Frank Lynch, ed., IPC Papers No. 2. Quezon City: Ateneo de Manila University Press, 1-21.

1964

Social Acceptance: Four Readings on Filipino Values. F. Lynch, ed. 2nd rev. ed. Quezon City: Ateneo de Manila University Press.

1972

"Social acceptance reconsidered." *IPC Papers No. 2. Four Readings on Philippine Values*. Frank Lynch and Alfonso de Guzman II, eds. (Fourth Edition, Enlarged). Quezon City: Ateneo de Manila University Press, 1973, 1-68.

Machado, Kit G.
1979

"Politics and dispute processing in rural Philippines." *Pacific Affairs 52*, 294-314.

McDermott Jr., John,
Wen-Shing Tseng and
Thomas Maretzki
1978

Peoples and Cultures of Hawaii: A Psychosocial Profile. Honolulu: John A. Burns School of Medicine and University of Hawaii Press.

Mangulabnan, Lito
1978

"Ang epekto ng paggamit ng wika at katayuan sa buhay sa pakikipag-ugnayan o N-aff ng ilang Pilipinong mag-aaral sa kolehiyo." ["The effect of language and social class on need affiliation among Filipino college students"]. *Ulat ng Ikatlong Pambansang Kumperensya sa Sikolohiyang Pilipino*. L.F. Antonio, Esther Reyes, Rogelia Pe & Nilda Almonte, eds. Lunsod Quezon: Pambansang Samahan sa Sikolohiyang Pilipino, 171-76.

Maningas, Ismael Irineo
1984

Contemporary Christian Morality in the Philippine Context. Manila: Research Center, De La Salle University.

Mataragnon, Rita H.
1987

"Pakikiramdam in Filipino social interaction." *Foundations of Behavioral Sciences: A Book of Readings*. Diliman, Quezon City: Social Science I Committee, University of the Philippines.

1984

"God of the rich, God of the poor." *Philippine Studies 32 (3-4), 5-26.*

Melendrez-Cruz, Patricia M.
1986

"From the Philippine Revolution, 1896 to military rule, 1972: The change in world-view in the Filipino short story." *Philippine World-View*. Virgilio G. Enriquez, ed. Heng Mui Keng Terrace, Pasis Penjang Singapore: Institute of Southeast Asian Studies.

Mercado, Leonardo
(ed.)
1977

Filipino Religious Psychology. Tacloban, Leyte: Divine Word University & Pambansang Samahan sa Sikolohiyang Pilipino.

Miranda, Dionisio M.
1987

Pagkamakatao: Reflections on the Theological Virtues in the Philippine Context. Manila: Divine Word Publications, 1-102.

Moghaddam, Fathali
M. and Donald M. Taylor
1987

"Towards appropriate training for developing world psychologists." *Growth and Progress in Cross-Cultural Psychology.* C. Kagitcibasi, ed., Lisse: Swets & Zeitlinger, 69-75.

Nofuente, Valerio
1979

"Portrayals of life and reality in radio and television drama." *Philippine World-View.* Virgilio G. Enriquez, ed. Heng Mui Keng Terrace, Pasis Penjang Singapore: Institute of Southeast Asian Studies, 1986.

1978

"Ang pananaw sa buhay na hatid ng drama at telebisyon" ["Portrayals of life and reality in radio and television]. *Ang Pandaigdigang Pananaw ng mga Pilipino* [The Pilipino Worldview]. Diliman, Quezon City: Philippine Psychology Research House.

Nuevo, Marilyn O.
1973

"Ang mga paksa, layunin at ekspresyong ginagamit sa paghuhuntahan ng mga Cebuana." *Sikolinggwistikang Pilipino.* Virgilio G. Enriquez, ed. Diliman, Quezon City: University of the Philippines, 53-60.

Okamura, Jonathan Y.
1987

"Filipino concepts of justice and the *Katarungang Pambarangay* system." *Kaya Tao 9* (1), 31-46. Journal of the Behavioral Sciences Department, De La Salle University.

Osias, Camilo
1940

The Filipino Way of Life: The Pluralized Philosophy. Boston: Ginn, 321 pp.

Panlasigui, Isidoro
1956
19__

Ti Ubing. La Union, Imprenta Evangelica, 45 pp.

Ti Agtutubo. Manila, Mission Press, 160 pp.

1951

Elementary Statistics & Educational Measurement & Evaluation. Manila: Community Publishers, 201 pp.

Pastores, Elizabeth A.
1981

"*Ang burges-komprador sa Pilipinas*: 1898-1941." *Philippine Social Sciences and Humanities Review XLV* (1-4), 313-32.

Panganiban, Jose Villa
and Consuelo Torres
Panganiban
1954

Panitikan ng Pilipinas. Lunsod Quezon: Bede's Publishing House, 284

Paular, Regino P.
1987

"Mental illness and the colonial order (1865-1898): An archival study." Unpublished thesis in Psychology, College of Social Sciences and Philosophy, University of the Philippines.

Pe-Pua, Rogelia E.,
(ed.)
1982

Filipino Psychology: Theory, Method and Application. Diliman, Quezon City: Philippine Psychology Research House, 352 pp.

1985

"*Ang pagtatanong-tanong: Katutubong metodo ng pananaliksik*" ["'Asking around': An indigenous research method"]. *Sikolohiyang Pilipino: Isyu, Pananaw at Kaalaman. (New Directions in Indigenous Psychology)*. Allen Agannon & S. Ma. Assumpta David, RVM, eds. Manila: National Book Store, Inc., 416-32.

[Philippines, Republic
of], Lupon sa Agham,
National Science
Development Board
(NSDB)
1970

Maugnayang Talasalitaang Pang-Agham, Ingles-Pilipino [*The "Maugnayin" Scientific English-Pilipino Vocabulary*]. Maynila: Lupon sa Agham. 185 pp.

Pike, Kenneth I.
1967

Language in Relation to a Unified Theory of the Structure of Human Behavior. The Hague: Mouton.

Ponce, Danilo E.
1980

"Introduction: The Philippine Background." *People and Cultures of Hawaii (A Psychocultural Profile)*. John F. McDermott Jr., Wen-Shing Tseng and Thomas W. Maretski, eds. Honolulu: John A. Burns School of Medicine and University of Hawaii Press, 155-63.

Quiazon, Serafin, Jr.
1973

"Personal at pormal na konsultasyon hinggil sa perspektibo ng sikolohiya sa Pilipinas para sa kasaysayan" (*Kasama si* A.V. Lagmay). Sulu Hotel, Lunsod Quezon, Nobyembre 1973.

Quisumbing, L. R.
1964N

"Child-rearing practices in the Cebuano extended family." *Philippine Sociological Review 12* (1-2), 109-14.

Rosales, Vicente
1965

"The influence of Spanish culture on the psychology of the Filipino." *Unitas 38* (4) 498-504.

Rubin, Joan
1976

"How to tell when someone is saying 'No.'" *Topics in Culture Learning*, 61-65.

Salazar, Zeus A.
1974

"Ang kultura, wika at kasaysayan." Interview during Psychology Week sponsored by the U.P. Psychological Society, Palma Hall, College of Arts and Sciences, University of the Philippines, August 2, 1974.

1981

"Wika at diwa: Isang pangsikolinggwistikang analisis sa halimbawa ng konsepto ng 'hiya' ["Language and consciousness: An illustrative psycholinguistic analysis of the concept of *'hiya'*"]. *Ulat ng Ikalabindalawang Seminar sa Sikolohiya ng Wika.* Susan Cipres-Ortega, ed.

Samonte, Elena
1973

"Kabuuan ng mga kahulugan ng mga salita sa larangang leksikal ng 'loob'" ["The meaning of the words in the lexical domain of 'loob'"]. Unpublished typescript. Diliman, Quezon City: University of the Philippines.

Samson, Jose A.
1965

"Is there a Filipino psychology?" *Unitas 38* (4), 447-87.

San Buenaventura, Mario
1983

"Ang pilosopikal na batayan ng sikolohiyang Pilipino." ["Philosophical basis of Filipino psychology"] M.A. (Psychology) thesis. University of the Philippines, Diliman, Quezon City.

Santiago, Carmen E.
1975
"Ang kahulugan ng pagkalalake sa mga Pilipino." *Sikolohiyang Pilipino: Mga Piling Papel.* Papel Blg. 4, Serye ng mga papel sa pagkataong Pilipino, Nobyembre 1975.

1976
"The language of food." *Culinary Culture of the Philippines.* Gilda F. Cordero, ed. Philippines: Bancom Audiovision Corporation, 133-39.

Santiago, Carmen E.
1977
"Pakapa-kapa: Paglilinaw ng isang konsepto sa nayon" ["*Pakapa-kapa*: Clarifying a concept in a rural setting"]. *Sikolohiyang Pilipino: Teorya, Metodo at Gamit (Filipino Psychology: Theory, Method and Application).* Rogelia Pe-Pua, ed. Lunsod Quezon: Surian ng Sikolohiyang Pilipino, Philippine Psychology Research and Training House, 1982, 161-70.

_____and
Virgilio G. Enriquez
1976
"Tungo sa makapilipinong pananaliksik" ["Towards a Filipino-oriented research"]. *Sikolohiyang Pilipino: Mga Ulat at Balita 1* (4), 3-10.

Santos, Emilino,
S. Flores at Rafael R.
Tavera
1985
Medicinal Plants: Mga Halamang Gamot. Manila: Philippine Book Co.

Santos, Jose P.
1935
Liwanag at Dilim: Buhay at mga Sinulat ni Emilio Jacinto. Paunang Salita ni Rafael Palma. Copyright 1935 by Dr. Jose P. Bantug. 97 pp.

Sato, Yusihiro
1988
"A Study of the Development of Pro-social Behavior." Unpublished M.A. Educational Psychology thesis, Graduate School of Education, University of Fukushima, Fukushima, Japan.

Serpell, Robert
1977
"Cultural validation of psychology." (A working paper for the emic/etic study group). Cross-cultural researcher's project/activity. Honolulu, Hawaii: East-West Center Culture Learning Institute, March 1977.

Sevilla, Judy C.
1978

"Indigenous research methods: evaluating first returns." *Sikolohiyang Pilipino: Teorya, Metodo at Gamit (Filipino Psychology: Theory, Method and Application)*. Rogelia Pe-Pua, ed. Lunsod Quezon: Surian ng Sikolohiyang Pilipino, Philippine Psychology Research and Training House, 1982, 221-32.

1985

"Evaluating indigenous methods: a second look." Unpublished paper. *Sikolohiyang Pilipino* roundtable discussion series, De La Salle University.

Sibley, W.
1965

Area Handbook on the Philippines. Human Relations Area Files, Inc., University of Chicago.

Silliman, G. Sidney
1982

"The folk legal culture of the Cebuano Filipino." *Philippine Quarterly of Culture and Society 10* (4), 225-44.

1983

"The Cebuano concept of justice." *Solidarity* no. 96, 21-28.

Sinha, Durganand
1984

"Psychology in rural areas: the case of a developing country." Invited address. International Congress of Psychology, Acapulco, Mexico, September 2-7.

Tan, Michael L.
1987

Usug, Kulam, Pasma: Traditional Concepts of Health and Illness in the Philippines. Quezon City: Alay Kapwa Kilusang Pangkalusugan (AKAP).

Temporal, A.J.
1968

"Some Filipino child-rearing practices and personality development." *Silliman Journal*.

Terada, Takifume
1987

"The Spirit Cult of Sto. Nino: An Anthropological Study of Popular Religiosity." Unpublished Ph. D (Anthropology) dissertation submitted to the Graduate School, College of Social Sciences and Philosophy, U.P. Diliman, Quezon City.

Tiston, Rebecca C.
1983

The Tambalans of Northern Leyte. Tacloban City, Philippines: Divine Word University Publications.

Torres, Edwin A.
1973

"Analysis of the meanings of 'yes' among Filipino college students." Typescript. Department of Psychology, University of the Philippines, October 6, 1973.

Triandis, H. C.
1972

The Analysis of Subjective Culture. New York: Wiley.

Velasco, Abraham B.
1975

"Ang kainginero: isang sosyo-sikolohikal na pagsusuri" ["The *kainginero*: a socio-psychological analysis"]. Unpublished M.A. (Psychology) thesis. Diliman, Quezon City: University of the Philippines.

Velazco, Gundelina Almario
1985

"Development of an instrument for the assessment of rural Filipino children's adaptive competence as an alternative to traditional intelligence measurement." *Philippine Journal of Educational Measurement 4* (1), 69-99.

1986

"Pagsusuri ng sikolohiya ni Francisco Baltazar 'Balagtas' sa Florante at Laura." Paper submitted to Dr. Virgilio G. Enriquez, Psychology 601, University of the Philippines, Diliman, Quezon City, March 14.

Ventura, Elizabeth
1973

"Ambiguity values of the Philippine Thematic Apperception Test (PTAT)." Unpublished M.A. thesis. Department of Psychology, University of the Philippines, Diliman, Quezon City, 153 pp.

1985

"Child psychology in the Philippines: some current trends." *Sikolohiyang Pilipino: Isyu, Pananaw at Kaalaman. (New Directions in Indigenous Psychology).* Allen Agannon & S. Ma. Assumpta David, RVM, eds. Manila: National Book Store, Inc., 512-30.

Wagatsuma, Hiroshi   *"Shudanshigi no Shinriteki Yooin"* [Psychologi-
1982   cal Factors in Collectivism'']. *Japanese Collectiv-
                                    ism.* Eshun Hamaguchi and Shunpei Kumon eds.
                                    Japan: Yuuhikaku, 1982. [Section 5: *Uchi to Soto*
                                    (In and Out)].

Watanabe, Fumio   ''The Japanese meets his Filipino counterpart at
1988   colleges and a state department in Philippine prov-
                                    inces.'' Special Symposium. ''The Changing Im-
                                    age of the Filipino.'' *Sikolohiyang Pilipino-Japan.*
                                    Indigenous Psychology Association. Tokyo, Japan
                                    Chapter. Kenshuto Auditorium, Komaba, Meguro
                                    Ku, Tokyo, Japan, August 19, 1988.

GLOSSARY

The following sources were consulted for the definitions found in this glossary; 1) *Diccionario Hispano-Tagalog* and *Diccionario Tagalog-Hispano* by Pedro Serrano-Laktaw, Manila, Estab. "La Opinion," a Cargo de G. Bautista, 1889-1914, 2) *Diksyunaryo Tesauro: Pilipino Ingles* by Jose Villa Panganiban, Manlapaz Publishing Co., Lunsod Quezon, Pilipinas, 1972; 3) *First Vicassan's Pilipino English Dictionary* by Vito C. Santos, Philippine Graphic Arts Inc., Caloocan City, 1978; 4) *Tagalog-English Dictionary* by Leo James English, Capitol Publishing House, Inc., 54 Don A. Roces Ave., Quezon City, 1986. Definitions without accompanying source/s were provided by the author.

amor propyo   [amor propio (Spanish).] self-esteem; self-love; pride.

English (1986): self-love; pride.

aswang   Panganiban (1972): a folkloric evil creature, capable of assuming diverse forms, and especially human form with horsefeet and horsetail.

English (1978): an evil creature supposed to be able to assume different forms and to harass people at night, esp. pregnant women.

bahala na   "Happen what may"; "We'll see"; determination; risk taking. (Colonial interpretation: fatalism).

Jose Panganiban (1972): We'll consider what to do when the time comes.

bayanihan   mutual aid; cooperative endeavor; cooperation; a community development.

bangungot   Panganiban (1972): n. nightmare. Syn. pangarap.

                       Santos (1978): n. nightmare. Syn. panaginip.

biro   n. joke; teasing; banter.

                       Serrano Laktaw (1914): Biru-biro kung sanlan, tutoo kung tamaan (Testing for a reaction)./Magbiro ka sa lasing, huag sa bagong gising (Joke with a drunk, not with one who just woke up)./Ang gawang pagbibiroan, kapatid nang tutohanan (Joking is from truth). [A more accurate translation would be "a joke is brother to the truth."]

                       Santos (1978): act of joking another; a joke, jest. Syn. tukso; tudyo; kantiyaw.

kabutihan   [r. w. buti (Tagalog). goodness; moral goodness or virtue; benevolence; something good that is done; kindness; an act of kindness; good; benefit; advantage; soundness; freedom from weakness or defect.

                       Santos (1978): being good or fine; excellence. Syn. husay; kahusayan; galing; inam; bentaha.

                       English (1986): goodness.

kalayaan   [r.w. laya.] n. freedom; liberty. (Elitist/reductionist version: social mobility).

                       Serrano Laktaw (1914): laya; kalayaan (libertad); emancipacion; Laya ng loob na makapamili at makagawa ng anoman; Albedrio, libre albedrio; ginhawa fam. Conveniencia; f.v.gr. Si Juan ay maibigin sa kaniyang kalayaan, Juan es amigo de su conveniencia.

                       Panganiban (1972): freedom; liberty; self autonomy; independence: kalayaan ng bansa/kalooban/isip sa takot.

                       Syn. pagsasarili; kasarinlan; independensya.

Santos (1978): freedom; liberty; independence; freedom to act on one's own free will; facility; libertinage; licentiousness. Syn. pagsasarili; kasarinlan; independensya. .

English (1986): Kalayaan ng kalooban (freedom of will)./Kalayaan sa pagsamba (freedom of worship).

kapayapaan

[r.w. payapa] n. Syn. katahimikan.

Santos (1978): peace; freedom from war; tranquillity; quiet.

English (1986): Kailan kaya magiging ganap ang kapayapaan? (When will peace be complete [perfect]?). Syn. katiwasayan; katahimikan.

kapwa

shared identity.

Serrano Laktaw (1914): kapowa. Los dos/Uno y otro; Una y otra./El uno y el otro, La una y la otra./

Ambos, bas, adj. pl./Igualmente adv. m. como adv. como adv. tawo. Semejante. adj. Projimo.

Siya'y kapowa ko tawo, el es hombre como yo; ibigin mo ang iyong kapowa o kapowa tawo, na para nang pagkaibig mo sa iyo rin, ama a tu projimo como a ti mismo. Pakikipagkapowa; pakikipagkapowa-tawo; karunungang makipagkapowa. Urbanidad; cortesania; sociabilidad. f. Marunong makipagkapowa. Urbano, na culto, ta cortes; social.

Panganiban (1972); both, fellow being. Kapwa bata/ tao./Mahalin ang kapwa./Tulungan ang kapwa.

Santos (1978): fellow being; other person
kapwa-tao: fellow human being like oneself.

English (1986): neighbor; fellow human being; fellowman. Dapat nating mahalin ang ating kapwa (we ought to love our fellowmen)./''Mahilig makipagkapwa'' (sociable; liking company). Syn. Kapwa-tao.

karangalan

dignity; honor. (Elitist/reductionist version: social acceptance).

Serrano Laktaw (1914): Dangal, karangalan. Honor. m. Honra; dignidad. f. Honradez. f. Sublimidad; suntuosidad. f. met. Credito; lauro; lustre. m. met. Corona. met. Alteza; eminencia; excelencia. f. Nagbibigay dangal; nagpaparangal. Honorifica, ca. adj.

marangal

Digno na; honrado, da; sobresaliente, sublime; suntuoso, sa. adj. met. Eminente; ilustre; egregio, ia adj. Real adj.=na gawa at nakapagbibigay puri.... Sinon. de bunyi; puri; sanghaya; unlak.

Santos (1978): honor, dignity; good name
Syn. puri; kapurihan; onor.

English (1986): [r.w. dangal.] honor; dignity;
Syn. puri; onor; dignidad.

karapatan

[r.w. dapat.]

Santos (1978): right or rights; privileges.

English (1986): right; privilege.
karapatang bomoto (right to vote). Syn. deretso; pribilehiyo; proper; appropriate.

katapatan

Panganiban (1972): sincerity; directness; frankness; loyalty.

Santos (1978): sincerity; frankness; honesty. Syn. pagkamatapat, pagkaprangka, kaprangkahan. Loyalty; faithfulness. Syn. pagkamatapat. Ant. kaliluhan, kataksilan, katraiduran. Truth; fact. Syn. katotohanan, pagkatotoo. Directness, as of a way or passage. Syn. katuwiran, kaderetsuhan.

English (1986): honesty, integrity, probity, uprightness, sincerity; freedom from pretense; constancy; faithfulness; allegiance; loyalty; fidelity; reliability; trustworthiness; uprightness; frankness; plainness of speech.

katarungan
[n. r. w. tarong (Cebuano).] justice; fairness. (Elitist/reductionist version: social equity).

Santos (1978): justice; sound reason; rightfulness; validity. Syn. katuwiran (impartiality; fairness).

English (1986): justice, equity. Dapat igawad ang katarungan (Justice must be done). Syn. Hustisya; pagkamamakatarungan; pagkakapantay-pantay. Ant. kawalang-katarungan (injustice); labag sa katarungan (contrary to justice); napaka-dimakatarungan (iniquitous, very unjust) pagbibigay katarungan (justifying; justification).

katotohanan
[r.w. totoo (Tagalog).] truth.

Panganiban (1972): Iba ang katotohanan sa katarungan. (The truth is different from reality.)/Ang katotohanan ay hindi nagbabago. (Truth never changes).

English (1986): Ang katotohanan kailanman ay di nagbabago. (Truth never changes).

katuwiran
[r.w. tuwid (Tagalog).] argument; reason; reasoning.

Panganiban (1972): katuwirang kakatwa (queer argument or reason)/katwirang linsad (off-tangent reasoning)/maykatwiran (is right).

English (1978): argument; reasoning; reason.

kulam
Santos (1978): n. witchcraft; witchery; sorcery.

Panganiban (1972): n. bewitchment; witchcraft.
Syn. gaway, ingkanto.

English (1986): ñ. sorcery; witchcraft; bewitchment
Syn. gaway; ohiya. V. kulamin/kumulam (to bewitch;
to enchant by witchcraft; to injure by witchcraft or
sorcery).

delikadesa [delicadeza (Spanish)] n. refinement; fastidiousness.
Syn. kadelikaduhan; kaselangan; pagkamaselan.

Santos (1978): fastidiousness; choosiness; prudishness; refinement.

English (1986): refinement; fastidiousness; prudishness.

engkanto [n. var. ingkanto/enkanto.]

English (1986): n. enchantment; charm; spell; a supernatural being (spirit). Syn. pagkagayuma.

Santos 1978. In Philippine folklore, a supernatural
being who has the power to enchant people.

gigil Panganiban (1972): trembling or thrill due to suppressed or irrepressible pleasure or liking.

Santos (1978): n. suppressed pleasure or thrill, sometimes anger, manifested by the gritting of the teeth.

English (1986): v.tremble or thrill from some
irrespressible emotion; gritting of the teeth because of
suppressed anger.

hangin n. wind; breeze; air.

Panganiban (1972): wind; breeze; air. "Masama sa
nilalagnat ang mahanginan (It is bad for one who has
fever to be exposed to the wind).

Santos (1978): wind; air; breeze.

hilot   n. local healer (colloquial).

Panganiban (1972): n. midwife. Syn. komadrona.

English (1986): midwife. Syn. manghihilot. v. to massage.

hiya   n. propriety; dignity. Syn. karangalan.

Serrano Laktaw (1914): Hiya; pagkahiya; paghiya; kahihiyan. Verguenza; afrenta. f. Cortedad; confusion. f. Rubor; rebozo; empacho; bochorno. m. = o paghabigo (sic: pagkabigo?). Chasco. m. malaki. met. Bofetada.... Sinon. de bikatalot; tukang. Ang taong kulang sa hiya, walang halaga ang wika (People don't rely on the words of a person without hiya).

Panganiban (1972): shame; embarrassment; timidity.

kahiyaan (an act that is demanded by face-saving or done in order not to lose honor); kahiya-hiya (shameful, embarrassing); kawalang-hiyaan (shamelessness).

English (1986): shame; a painful feeling of having done something wrong, improper or silly; disgrace; anything that causes shame; humiliation; dishonor; ignominy; reproach; a cause of blame and disgrace: anything that causes shame. Hiya; hiyain; humiya; nang hiya; hiyanghiya; ikahiya; ipagmakahiya.

hiyang   adj. suited; compatible; aggreable (eg. climate, food, etc.) Syn. agpang; akma; tama.

Panganiban (1972): agreeing (as medicine, food, etc.).

Santos (1978): n. agreeableness or suitability to one's health or physical constitution.

English (1986): adj. suited, compatible. Syn. angkop; tama; bagay; agpang.

lambing   n. sweetness; caress (not necessarily physical).

Serrano Laktaw (1914): Lambing. Mimo; regalo; chiqueo. m. fam. Antojo. m. Malambing. Mimoso, sa; regalon, na. adj. Maglambing. Mimar. Chiquear. a. Antojarse; encapricharse. r. Sinon de wingwing.

English: caress, showing fondness; affection or tenderness; Syn. karinyo.

Santos (1978): show or expression of fondness, or tenderness, as by embracing, kissing; the characteristic attitude of a child wanting to be caressed or fondled.

loob   n. interior aspect of kapwa; shared inner self.

Panganiban (1972): interior; internal part; the inside; courage; valor. Syn. tapang; giting.

Santos (1978): inside; interior; inner part.

loobin   Panganiban (1972): one's state of mind; disposition.

Syn. kalooban; kagustuhan.

kagandahang loob   shared humanity.

Panganiban (1972): generosity. Syn. kabutihang-loob; pagkamatulungin.

lakas ng loob   guts.

Serrano Laktaw (1914): Lakas m. nang loob, valor, animo: corazon coraje. m. Resolucion. f. Lakas-loob!

Animo!

sama ng loob   resentment.

Serrano Laktaw (1914): sama-samaan (nang loob). Digusto; pique; sentimiento; resentimiento. m. de sama.

utang na loob   appreciation of kapwa solidarity.

Serrano Laktaw (1914): Utang na loob; pautang na loob. Favor.m. Amparo; socorro. m. Magkautang nang loob. Deber favores o attenciones. Pautangan; o pautangin nang loob; Hacer favor.Socorrer; favorecer; amparar; ayudar; auxiliar; proteger....(Note: All the four sayings given by Laktaw are on utang and not on utang na loob). Syn. interyor, will; state of mind; volition disposition. Syn. tapang; giting; lakas ng loob. Manners: behavior. Syn. asal; ugali.

malimali   [n. var. mali-mali.]

Santos (1978): senile: subject to mistakes and absent-mindedness of old age. Syn. huli, ulianin.

English (1986): adj. senile; prone to make mistakes because of old age.

mañana habit   [mañana (Spanish); habit (English).] procrastination.

English (1986): procrastination.

ngilo   Panganiban (1972): pain felt at tooth edge.

Santos (1978): sensation of tingling discomfort on the edges of the teeth.

English (1986): putting the teeth on edge: nerve pain at edge of the tooth.

paki-/pakiki   Prefix forming nouns to denote shared humanity/favor/request/sympathetic sharing/rapport/cooperation.

pakikibaka   cooperative resistance.

pakikisama   yielding to the leader or majority; companionship; esteem; "after-fellow."

pakiramdam   shared inner perception; feeling for another; sensing cues.

	Serrano Laktaw (1914): Dama pagdama; pagdarama; pandarama. Tacto; tiento; tocamiento; palpamiento.... Damdam pangdamdam. Sentido; sentir...pakiramdaman; makiramdam. Escuchar; atender.
pasma	Panganiban (1972): spasm. Syn. ngimay; kalambre; pamimitig; ngalay; kislig.

Santos (1978): an abnormal state of the nerves with manifestation of sweating and slight shaking of the body or any part of it esp. the hands.

English (1986): n. spasm. Syn. panginginig. |
| *sikolohiyang Pilipino* | [psicologia (Spanish).] Filipino psychology. |
| *sumpong* | whim; caprice; sudden change of mind without any reason; surge of mild lunacy. |
| *tampo* | n. affective disappointment; unmet expectations.

Panganiban (1972): n. act of sulking; matampuhin-- prone to be sulky.

Santos (1978): n. resentment; ill humor shown by a sullen, withdrawn behavior.

English (1986): n. sulkiness; huff; peevishness; displeasure; slight anger; complaint against someone for their lack of attention. |

INDEX